MOUNTAIN BIKE
INDIANA

MOUNTAIN BIKE INDIANA

© 1996 by Layne Cameron. All rights reserved. No part of this book may be reproduced in any form without the written permission of the publisher or author.

Maps created by Beachway Press
Illustrations by Mike Francis and Dean Stanton
Photographs by Layne Cameron
Consulting editor, John Phillips

ISBN 1-882997-05-0

Library of Congress Cataloging-in-Publication Data
    Cameron, Layne
    Mountain Bike Indiana: An Atlas of Indiana's Greatest Off-Road Bicycle
Rides / by Layne Cameron. 1st ed. Springfield, VA : Beachway Press, ©1996.
    224 pages : Illustrations, Photographs, Maps
        1. All-terrain cycling—Indiana—Guidebooks.
Indiana—Guidebooks.
95-083782
CIP

Published by Beachway Press
9201 Beachway Lane
Springfield, VA 22153-1441

Printed in the United States of America
Automated Graphic Systems, Inc.

10 9 8 7 6 5 4 3 2 1

MOUNTAIN BIKE
INDIANA

An Atlas of Indiana's Greatest Off-Road Bicycle Rides

by Layne Cameron

Introduction by Scott Adams, Series Editor

Beachway Press

An addition to

Beachway Press' **Mountain Bike America** *Series*

Dear Readers:
Every effort was made to make this the most accurate, informative, and easy-to-use guidebook on the planet. Any comments, suggestions, and corrections regarding this guide or any of its rides are welcome and should be sent to:

Beachway Press
c/o Editorial Dept.
9201 Beachway Lane
Springfield, VA 22153

We'd love to hear from you so we can make future editions and future guides even better.

Thanks and happy trails!

Table of Contents

Preface

Mountain biking notwithstanding, what I enjoy most about loading up the truck and wandering out into the woods is the conversations around the campfire— in-depth, uninhibited, with time being measured not by a watch, but by a dying campfire. Huddled around the glowing embers, topics of discussion cover relationships, religion, goals, observations, nostalgia, and—of course—mountain biking.

One particular night, as the cold began to overwhelm our circle, the conversations tapered off and sleep became imminent. I wandered off to bed and soon my body began to heat up my sleeping bag. I began to relax. Lying on a cot under a sky that was riddled with stars and listening to a nearby owl's one-question lullaby, my mind began to review this past year and the time that was spent working on the book and becoming intimate with my home state.

Granted, Indiana's topography is somewhat limited. Thanks to the work of many glaciers, two-thirds of the state was cleared flat. Today, much of the land is used for farming, but those giant ice bulldozers did leave a few hilly moraines and kettle holes in the north. In most cases, the trail systems to the north make the most of these limited flaws on the topography. Trails circle shallow reservoirs, edge the sand dunes of Lake Michigan, or coil up and down a solitary hill before rolling into a surrounding field.

What these trails might lack in severity, they make up for with interesting histories. For example, following a portion of Indiana's northernmost trail, a man trundled across the state on a high-wheeler on his quest to ride around the world. Another loop serves as the model for all state-owned property, representing area cyclists' quest to gain access to more trails. And in Kokomo, a bike shop has been in business longer than most of us have been alive, yet one man has been at the helm for all but three years of the shop's existence.

Traveling down to the southern part of the state, one can see where the glaciers ended their trek and dumped their load. They upturned the soil and brought top-grade coal and limestone near the surface. Quarries and coal mines mark these easy-access extraction sites and interrupt the miles of rolling forest that sit atop this crumpled land. During the summer, the steam that settles between its ridges creates an Appalachian scene that inspires books and leads many to call this area the "Little Smokies."

Here, the trails lead past Native American ceremonial sites, historical markers documenting Civil War skirmishes, and towns with names like Story, Stonehead, Oolitic, Hindostan, and Gnaw Bone. Neighbors include deer, grouse, pileated and blackback woodpeckers, owls, wild turkey, grouse, mink, skunks, and skinks. Limestone shelves serve as benches to offer a break from the granny-gear grinding climbs, as well as a place to think about the forthcoming fork-bending descents.

As I rolled over in my sleeping bag, I thought about the wear on my body and equipment—and the subsequent trips to the doctor and bike mechanic. I recalled the steroid shots for the two major bouts of poison ivy, warming numb toes by the campfire, drinking gallons of water to drown out the heat exhaustion, barely controlling my arachnophobia as I picked spiders and webs off my face, charring the butts of ticks to entice them out of my skin, overhauling my bike four times, and replacing countless numbers of tubes.

In the zone between consciousness and dreaming, I remembered the people I've met while completing the mapping, research, writing, and riding. They include the rangers who patrol the forest and maintain the trails, the political leaders fighting for land access and rails-to-trails corridors, the equestrians I've shared campsites with, the concerned hunter who lent me a bright orange cap, the select few I've shared fire pizzas and ale with, the ranger who gave me a ride back to my truck after I flatted without a spare, the motherly innkeepers at the bed and breakfasts, and all the cyclists who shared their trails with me.

After reviewing the condition of the state's mountain biking, I drifted off with the understanding that I am merely a messenger. I have documented the work of the people who fought to keep land open, physically constructed the trails, and have made many sacrifices so that others can enjoy their work. When I wake, I will tread softly upon the trails that they have created and enjoy another great day—mountain biking in Indiana.

— Layne Cameron

Acknowledgments

A special thanks to Beachway Press for paying me to travel around seemingly every two-lane highway and ride every singletrack trail in the Hoosier state. What a great feeling it was to combine my writing profession with my cycling obsession.

Thanks to Matt Carrel at Chico's Bike Shop for providing mechanical support for the entire mountain bike tour. To everyone at the Hoosier National Forest Office for guiding me to the greatest trails in the state.

Special thanks to Cliff Johnson of the Indiana Bicycle Coalition and the area directors. Thanks to all the guys who helped guide me and accompanied me through the singletrack: Steve George, Ron Pendley, Curt Jones, Don Gary, Bob Brooks, Richard Ries, Chris Arvin, Charlie McClary, Brent Mullen, and Steve Mullin.

Thanks to Gretchen and everyone else at the Story Inn for a luxurious stay and some incredible food. Also to everyone at the Cliff House for a great weekend and an incredible hilltop view of the Ohio River.

Special thanks to Sandy Grieshop for her helpful editing and encouragement.

Thanks to my parents and friends for their support and willingness to allow me to wander off, weekend after weekend. And to my son, Alex, who will someday ride these great trails with me.

Introduction

Welcome to the new generation of bicycling! Indeed, the sport has evolved dramatically from the thin-tired, featherweight-frame days of old. The sleek geometry and lightweight frames of racing bicycles, still the heart and soul of bicycling worldwide, have lost much ground in recent years, unpaving the way for the mountain bike, which now accounts for the majority of all bicycle sales in the U.S. And with this change comes a new breed of cyclist, less concerned with smooth roads and long rides, who thrives in places once inaccessible to the mortal road bike.

The mountain bike, with its knobby tread and reinforced frame, takes cyclists to places once unheard of—down rugged mountain trails, through streams of rushing water and thick mud, across the frozen Alaskan tundra, and even to work in the city. There seem to be few limits on what this fat-tired beast can do and where it can take us. Few obstacles stand in its way, few boundaries slow its progress. Except for one—its own success. If trail closure means little to you now, read on and discover how a trail can be here today and gone tomorrow. With so many new off-road cyclists taking to the trails each year, its no wonder trail access hinges precariously between universal acceptance and complete termination. But a little work on your part can go a long way to preserving trail access for future use. Nothing is more crucial to the survival of mountain biking itself than to read the examples set forth in the following pages and practice their message. Then turn to the maps, pick out your favorite ride, and hit the dirt!

WHAT THIS BOOK IS ABOUT

Within these pages you will find everything you need to know about off-road bicycling in the state of Indiana. This guidebook begins by exploring the fascinating history of the mountain bike itself, then goes on to discuss everything from the health benefits of off-road cycling to tips and techniques for bicycling over logs and up hills. Also included are the types of clothing to keep you comfortable and in style, essential equipment ideas to keep your rides smooth and trouble-free, and descriptions of off-road terrain to prepare you for the kinds of bumps and bounces you can expect to encounter. The two major provisions of this book, though, are its unique and detailed maps and relentless dedication to trail preservation.

Each of the 28 rides included in this book is accompanied by four very different maps. A **location map** shows where each ride is in relation to the rest of Indiana; the **3D profile map** displays an accurate view of the each ride's ups and downs in three dimensions, the **road map** leads you through each ride and is accompanied by detailed directions, and a **3D surface area map** provides a fascinating view of the surrounding topography and landscape.

Without open trails, the maps in this book are virtually useless. Cyclists must learn to be responsible for the trails they use and to share these trails with others. This guidebook addresses such issues as why trail use has become so controversial, what can be done to improve the image of mountain biking, how to have fun and ride responsibly, on-the-spot trail repair techniques, trail maintenance hotlines for each trail, and the worldwide-standard *Rules of the Trail*.

Each of the 28 rides is complete with maps, trail descriptions and directions, local history, and a quick-reference information board including such items as trail-maintenance hotlines, park schedules, costs, and alternative maps.

It's important to note that mountain bike rides tend to take longer than road rides because the average speed is often much slower. Average speeds can vary from a climbing pace of three to four miles per hour to 12 to 13 miles per hour on flatter roads and trails. Keep this in mind when planning your trip.

MOUNTAIN BIKE BEGINNINGS

It seems the mountain bike, originally designed for lunatic adventurists bored with straight lines, clean clothes, and smooth tires, has become globally popular in as short a time as it would take to race down a mountain trail.

Like many things of a revolutionary nature, the mountain bike was born

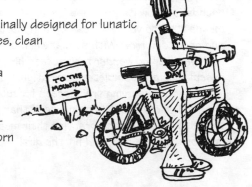

on the west coast. But unlike Rollerblades, purple hair, and the peace sign, the concept of the off-road bike cannot be credited solely to the imaginative Californians—they were just the first to make waves.

The design of the first off-road specific bike was based on the geometry of the old Schwinn Excelsior, a one-speed, camel-back cruiser with balloon tires. Joe Breeze was the creator behind it, and in 1977 he built 10 of these "Breezers" for himself and his Marin County, California, friends at $750 apiece—a bargain.

Breeze was a serious competitor in bicycle racing, placing 13th in the 1977 U.S. Road Racing National Championships. After races, he and friends would scour local bike shops hoping to find old bikes they could then restore.

It was the 1941 Schwinn Excelsior, for which Breeze paid just five dollars, that began to shape and change bicycling history forever. After taking the bike home, removing the fenders, oiling the chain, and pumping up the tires, Breeze hit the dirt. He loved it.

His inspiration, while forerunning was not altogether unique. On the opposite end of the country, nearly 2,500 miles from Marin County, east coast bike bums were also growing restless. More and more old, beat-up clunkers were being restored and modified. These behemoths often weighed as much as 80 pounds and were so reinforced they seemed virtually indestructible. But rides that take just 40 minutes on today's 25-pound featherweights took the steel-toed-boot- and-blue-jean-clad bikers of the late 1970s and early 1980s nearly four hours to complete.

Not until 1981 was it possible to purchase a production mountain bike, but local retailers found these ungainly bicycles difficult to sell and rarely kept them in stock. By 1983, however, mountain bikes were no longer such a fringe item, and large bike manufacturers quickly jumped into the action, producing their own versions of the off-road bike. By the 1980s, the mountain bike had firmly established its place with bicyclists of nearly all ages and abilities, and now command nearly 00 percent of the U.S. bike market.

There are many reasons for the mountain bike's success in becoming the hottest two-wheeled vehicle in the nation. They are much friendlier to the cyclist than traditional road bikes because of their comfortable upright position and shock-absorbing fat tires. And because of the health-conscious, environmentalist movement of the late 1980s and 1990s, people are more activity minded and seek nature on a closer front than paved roads can allow. The mountain bike gives you these things and takes you far away from the daily grind—even if you're only minutes from the city.

MOUNTAIN BIKING INTO SHAPE

If your objective is to get in shape and lose weight, then you're on the right track, because mountain biking is one of the best ways to get started.

One way many of us have lost weight in this sport is the crash-and-burn-it-off method. Picture this: you're speeding uncontrollably down a vertical drop that you realize you shouldn't be on—only after it is too late. Your front wheel lodges into a rut and launches you through endless weeds, trees, and pointy rocks before coming to an abrupt halt in a puddle of thick mud. Surveying the damage, you discover, with the layers of skin, body parts, and lost confidence littering the trail above, that those unwanted pounds have been shed—permanently. Instant weight loss.

There is, of course, a more conventional (and quite a bit less painful) approach to losing weight and gaining fitness on a mountain bike. It's called the workout, and bicycles provide an ideal way to get physical. Take a look at some of the benefits associated with cycling.

Cycling helps you shed pounds without gimmicky diet fads or weight-loss programs. You can explore the countryside and burn nearly 10 to 16 calories per minute or close to 600 to 1,000 calories per hour. Moreover, it's a great way to spend an afternoon.

No less significant than the external and cosmetic changes of your body from riding are the internal changes taking place. Over time, cycling regularly will strengthen your heart as your body grows vast networks of new capillaries to carry blood to all those working muscles. This will, in turn, give your skin a healthier glow. The capacity of your lungs may increase up to 20 percent, and your resting heart rate will drop significantly. The Stanford University School of Medicine reports to the American Heart Association that people can reduce their risk of heart attack by nearly 64 percent if they can burn up to 2,000 calories per week. This is only two to three hours of bike riding!

Recommended for insomnia, hypertension, indigestion, anxiety, and even for recuperation from major heart attacks, bicycling can be an excellent cure-all as well as a great preventive. Cycling just a few hours per week can improve your figure and sleeping habits, give you greater resistance to illness, increase your energy levels, and provide feelings of accomplishment and heightened self-esteem.

BE SAFE—KNOW THE LAW

Occasionally, even the hard-core off-road cyclists will find they have no choice but to ride the pavement. When you are forced to hit the road, it's important for you to know and understand the rules.

Outlined below are a few of the common laws found in Indiana's Vehicle Code book.

- **Bicycles are legally classified as vehicles in the state of Indiana**. This means that as a bicyclist, you are responsible for obeying the same rules of the road as a driver of a motor vehicle.
- **Bicyclists must ride with the traffic—*NOT AGAINST IT!*** Because bicycles are considered vehicles, you must ride your bicycle just as you would drive a

car—with traffic. Only pedestrians should travel against the flow of traffic.

- **You must obey all traffic signs**. This includes stop signs and stoplights.

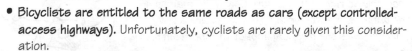

- **Always signal your turns**. Most drivers aren't expecting bicyclists to be on the roads, and many drivers would prefer that cyclists stay off the roads altogether. It's important, therefore, to clearly signal your intentions to motorists both in front and behind you.

- **Bicyclists are entitled to the same roads as cars (except controlled-access highways)**. Unfortunately, cyclists are rarely given this consideration.

- **Be a responsible cyclist**. Do not abuse your rights to ride on open roads. Follow the rules and set a good example for all of us as you roll along.

THE MOUNTAIN BIKE CONTROVERSY

Are Mountain Bicyclists Environmental Outlaws?
Do We have the Right to Use Public Trails?

Mountain bikers have long endured the animosity of folks in the backcountry who complain about the consequences of off road bicycling. Many people believe that the fat tires and knobby tread do unacceptable environmental damage and that our uncontrollable riding habits are a danger to animals and to other trail users. To the contrary, mountain bikes have no more environmental impact than hiking boots or horseshoes. This does not mean, however, that mountain bikes leave no imprint at all. Wherever man treads, there is an impact. By riding responsibly, though, it is possible to leave only a minimum impact—something we all must take care to achieve.

Unfortunately, it is often people of great influence who view the mountain bike as the environment's worst enemy. Consequently, we as mountain bike riders and environmentally concerned citizens must be educators, impressing upon others that we also deserve the right to use these trails. Our responsibilities as bicyclists are no more and no less than any other trail user. We must all take the soft-cycling approach and show that mountain bicyclists are not environmental outlaws.

ETIQUETTE OF MOUNTAIN BIKING

Moving softly across the land means leaving no more than an echo.
                                                          Hank Barlow

When discussing mountain biking etiquette, we are in essence discussing the soft-cycling approach. This term, as mentioned previously, describes the art of minimum-impact bicycling and should apply to both the physical and social dimensions of the sport. But make no mistake—it is possible to ride fast and furiously while maintaining the balance of soft-cycling. Here first are a few ways to minimize the physical impact of mountain bike riding.

- **Stay on the trail**. Don't ride around fallen trees or mud holes that block your path. Stop and cross over them. When you come to a vista overlooking a deep valley, don't ride off the trail for a better vantage point. Instead, leave the bike and walk to see the view. Riding off the trail may seem inconsequential when done only once, but soon someone else will follow, then others, and the cumulative results can be catastrophic. Each time you wander from the trail you begin creating a new path, adding one more scar to the earth's surface.
- **Do not disturb the soil**. Follow a line within the trail that will not disturb or damage the soil.
- **Do not ride over soft or wet trails**. After a rain shower or during the thawing season, trails will often resemble muddy, oozing swampland. The best thing to do is stay off the trails altogether. Realistically, however, we're all going to come across some muddy trails we cannot anticipate. Instead of blasting through each section of mud, which may seem both easier and more fun, lift the bike and walk past. Each time a cyclist rides through a soft or muddy section of trail, that part of the trail is permanently damaged. Regardless of the trail's conditions, though, remember always to go over the obstacles across the path, **NOT AROUND THEM**. Stay on the trail.
- **Avoid trails that, for all but God, are considered impassable and impossible**. Don't take a leap of faith down a kamikaze descent on which you will be forced to lock your brakes and skid to the bottom, ripping the ground apart as you go.

Soft-cycling should apply to the social dimensions of the sport as well, since mountain bikers are not the only folks who use the trails. Hikers, equestrians, cross-country skiers, and other outdoors people use many of the same trails and can be easily spooked by a marauding mountain biker tearing through the trees. Be friendly in the forest and give ample warning of your approach.

- **Take out what you bring in.** Don't leave broken bike pieces and banana peels scattered along the trail.
- **Be aware of your surroundings.** Don't use popular hiking trails for race training.
- **Slow down!** Rocketing around blind corners is a sure way to ruin an unsuspecting hiker's day. Consider this—If you fly down a quick singletrack descent at 20 mph, then hit the brakes and slow down to only six mph to pass someone, you're still moving twice as fast as they are!

Like the trails we ride on, the social dimension of mountain biking is very fragile and must be cared for responsibly. We should not want to destroy another person's enjoyment of the outdoors. By riding in the backcountry with caution, control, and responsibility, our presence should be felt positively by other trail users. By adhering to these rules, trail riding—a privilege that can quickly be taken away—will continue to be ours to share.

TRAIL MAINTENANCE

Unfortunately, despite all of the preventive measures taken to avoid trail damage, we're still going to run into many trails requiring attention. Simply put, a lot of hikers, equestrians, and cyclists alike use the same trails—some wear and tear is unavoidable. But like your bike, if you want to use these trails for a long time to come, you must also maintain them.

Trail maintenance and restoration can be accomplished in a variety of ways. One way is for mountain bike clubs to combine efforts with other trail users (i.e. hikers and equestrians) and work closely with land managers to cut new trails or repair existing ones. This not only reinforces to others the commitment cyclists have in caring for and maintaining the land, but also breaks the ice that often separates cyclists from their fellow trailmates. Another good way to help out is to show up on a Saturday morning with a few riding buddies at your favorite off-road domain ready to work. With a good attitude, thick gloves, and the local land manager's supervision, trail repair is fun and very rewarding. It's important, of course, that you arrange a trail-repair outing with the local land manager before you start pounding shovels into the dirt. They can lead you to the most needy sections of trail and instruct you on what repairs should be done and how best to accomplish the task. Perhaps the most effective means of trail maintenance, though, can be done by yourself and while you're riding. Read on.

ON-THE-SPOT QUICK FIX

Most of us, when we're riding, have at one time or another come upon muddy trails or fallen trees blocking our path. We notice that over time the mud gets deeper and the trail gets wider as people go through or around the obstacles. We worry that the problem will become so severe and repairs too difficult that the trail's access may be threatened. We also know that our ambition to do anything about it is greatest at that moment, not after a hot shower and plate of spaghetti. Here are a few on-the-spot quick fixes you can do that will hopefully correct a problem before it gets out of hand and get you back on your bike within minutes.

- **MUDDY TRAILS.** What do you do when trails develop huge mud holes destined for the EPA's Superfund status? The technique is called corduroying, and it works much like building a pontoon over the mud to support bikes, horses, or hikers as they cross. Corduroy (not the pants) is the term for roads made of logs laid down crosswise. Use small-and medium-sized sticks and lay them side by side across the trail until they cover the length of the muddy section (break the sticks to fit the width of the trail). Press them into the mud with your feet, then lay more on top if needed. Keep adding sticks until the trail is firm. Not only will you stay clean as you cross, but the sticks may soak up some of the water and help the puddle dry. This quick fix may last as long as one month before needing to be redone. And as time goes on, with new layers added to the trail, the soil will grow stronger, thicker, and more resistant to erosion. This whole process may take fewer than five minutes, and you can be on your way, knowing the trail behind you is in good repair.

- **LEAVING THE TRAIL.** What do you do to keep cyclists from cutting corners and leaving the designated trail? The solution is much simpler than you may think. (No, don't hire an off-road police force.) Notice where people are leaving the trail and throw a pile of thick branches or brush along the path, or place logs across the opening to block the way through. There are probably dozens of subtle tricks like these that will manipulate people into staying on the designated trail. If executed well, no one will even notice that the thick branches scattered along the ground in the woods weren't always there. And most folks would probably rather take a moment to hop a log in the trail than get tangled in a web of branches.

- **OBSTACLES IN THE WAY.** If there are large obstacles blocking the trail, try and remove them or push them aside. If you cannot do this by yourself, call the trail maintenance hotline to speak with the land manager of that particular trail and see what can be done.

We have to be willing to sweat *for* our trails in order to sweat *on* them. Police yourself and point out to others the significance of trail maintenance. "Sweat Equity," the rewards of continued land use won with a fair share of sweat, pays off when the trail is "up for review" by the land manager and he or she remembers the efforts made by trail conscious mountain bikers.

RULES OF THE TRAIL

The International Mountain Bicycling Association (IMBA) has developed these guidelines to trail riding. These "Rules of the Trail" are accepted worldwide and will go a long way in keeping trails open. Please respect and follow these rules for everyone's sake.

1. **Ride only on open trails.** Respect trail and road closures (if you're not sure, ask a park or state official first), do not trespass on private property, and obtain permits or authorization if required. Federal and state wilderness areas are off-limits to cycling. Parks and state forests may also have certain trails closed to cycling.
2. **Leave no trace.** Be sensitive to the dirt beneath you. Even on open trails, you should not ride under conditions by which you will leave evidence of your passing, such as on certain soils or shortly after a rainfall. Be sure to observe the different types of soils and trails you're riding on, practicing minimum-impact cycling. Never ride off the trail, don't skid your tires, and be sure to bring out at least as much as you bring in.
3. **Control your bicycle!** Inattention for even one second can cause disaster for yourself or for others. Excessive speed frightens and can injure people, gives mountain biking a bad name, and can results in trail closures.
4. **Always yield.** Let others know you're coming well in advance (a friendly greeting is always good and often appreciated). Show your respect when passing others by slowing to walking speed or

BICYCLES YIELD TO PEDESTRIANS

stopping altogether, especially in the presence of horses. Horses can be unpredictable, so be very careful. Anticipate that other trail users may be around corners or in blind spots.

5. **Never spook animals**. All animals are spooked by sudden movements, unannounced approaches, or loud noises. Give the animals extra room and time so they can adjust to you. Move slowly or dismount around animals. Running cattle and disturbing wild animals are serious offenses. Leave gates as you find them, or as marked.

6. **Plan ahead.** Know your equipment, your ability, and the area in which you are riding, and plan your trip accordingly. Be self-sufficient at all times, keep your bike in good repair, and carry necessary supplies for changes in weather or other conditions. You can help keep trails open by setting an example of responsible, courteous, and controlled mountain bike riding.

7. **Always wear a helmet when you ride**. For your own safety and protection, a helmet should be worn whenever you are riding your bike. You never know when a tree root or small rock will throw you the wrong way and send you tumbling.

According to Responsible Organized Mountain Pedalers (ROMP) of Campbell, California, "thousands of miles of dirt trails have been closed to mountain bicycling because of the irresponsible riding habits of just a few riders." Don't follow the example of these offending riders. Don't take away trail privileges from thousands of others who work hard each year to keep the backcountry avenues open to us all.

THE NECESSITIES OF CYCLING

When discussing the most important items to have on a bike ride, cyclists generally agree on the following four items.

- **HELMET.** The reasons to wear a helmet should be obvious. Helmets are discussed in more detail in the *Be Safe—Wear Your Armor* section.
- **WATER**. Without it, cyclists may face dehydration, which may result in dizziness and fatigue. On a warm day, cyclists should drink at least one full bottle during every hour of riding. Remember, it's always good to drink before you feel thirsty—otherwise, it may be too late.
- **CYCLING SHORTS**. These are necessary if you plan to ride your bike more than 20 to 30 minutes. Padded cycling shorts may be the only thing preventing your derriere from serious saddle soreness by ride's end. There are two types of cycling shorts you can buy. Touring shorts are good for people who don't want to look like they're wearing anatomically correct cellophane. These look like regular athletic shorts with pockets, but have built-in padding in the crotch area for protection from chafing and saddle sores. The more popular, traditional cycling shorts are made of skin-tight

material, also with a padded crotch. Whichever style you find most comfortable, cycling shorts are a necessity for long rides.

- **FOOD.** This essential item will keep you rolling. Cycling burns up a lot of calories and is among the few sports in which no one is safe from the "Bonk." Bonking feels like it sounds. Without food in your system, your blood sugar level collapses, and there is no longer any energy in your body. This instantly results in total fatigue and light-headedness. So when you're filling your water bottle, remember to bring along some food. Fruit, energy bars, or some other forms of high-energy food are highly recommended. Candy bars are not, however, because they will deliver a sudden burst of high energy, then let you down soon after, causing you to feel worse than before. Energy bars are available at most bike stores and are similar to candy bars, but provide complex carbohydrate energy and high nutrition rather than the fast-burning simple sugars of candy bars.

BE PREPARED OR DIE

Essential equipment that will keep you from dying alone in the woods:

- SPARE TUBE
- TIRE IRONS — See the *Appendix* for instructions on fixing flat tires.
- PATCH KIT
- PUMP
- MONEY — Spare change for emergency calls.
- SPOKE WRENCH
- SPARE SPOKES — To fit your wheel. Tape these to the chain stay.
- CHAIN TOOL
- ALLEN KEYS — Bring appropriate sizes to fit your bike.
- COMPASS
- FIRST AID KIT
- MATCHES
- GUIDEBOOK — In case all else fails and you must start a fire to survive, the guidebook will serve as excellent fire starter!

To carry these items, you may need a bike bag. A bag mounted in front of the handlebars provides quick access to your belongings, whereas a saddle bag fitted underneath the saddle keeps things out of your way. If you're carrying lots of equipment, you may want to consider a set of panniers. These are much larger and mount on either side of each wheel. Many cyclists, though, prefer not to use a bag at all. They just slip all they need into their jersey pockets, and off they go.

BE SAFE—WEAR YOUR ARMOR

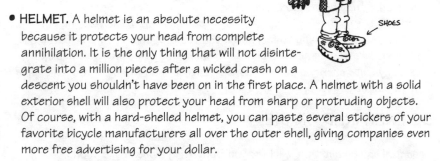

While on the subject of jerseys, it's crucial to discuss the clothing you must wear to be safe, practical, and—if you prefer—stylish. The following is a list of items that will save you from disaster, outfit you comfortably, and most important, keep you looking cool.

- **HELMET.** A helmet is an absolute necessity because it protects your head from complete annihilation. It is the only thing that will not disintegrate into a million pieces after a wicked crash on a descent you shouldn't have been on in the first place. A helmet with a solid exterior shell will also protect your head from sharp or protruding objects. Of course, with a hard-shelled helmet, you can paste several stickers of your favorite bicycle manufacturers all over the outer shell, giving companies even more free advertising for your dollar.

- **SHORTS.** Let's just say Lycra cycling shorts are considered a major safety item if you plan to ride for more than 20 or 30 minutes at a time. As mentioned in *The Necessities of Cycling* section, cycling shorts are well regarded as the leading cure-all for chafing and saddle sores. The most preventive cycling shorts have padded "chamois" (most chamois is synthetic nowadays) in the crotch area. Of course, if you choose to wear these traditional cycling shorts, it's imperative that they look as if someone spray painted them onto your body.

- **GLOVES.** You may find well-padded cycling gloves invaluable when traveling over rocky trails and gravelly roads for hours on end. Long-fingered gloves may also be useful, as branches, trees, assorted hard objects, and, occasionally, small animals will reach out and whack your knuckles.

- **GLASSES.** Not only do sunglasses give you an imposing presence and make you look cool (both are extremely important), they also protect your eyes from harmful ultraviolet rays, invisible branches, creepy bugs, dirt, and may prevent you from being caught sneaking glances at riders of the opposite sex also wearing skintight, revealing Lycra.

- **SHOES.** Mountain bike shoes should have stiff soles to help make pedaling easier and provide better traction when walking your bike up a trail becomes necessary. Virtually any kind of good outdoor hiking footwear will work, but specific mountain bike shoes (especially those with inset cleats) are best. It is vital that these shoes look as ugly as humanly possible. Those closest in style to bowling shoes are, of course, the most popular.

- **JERSEY or SHIRT.** Bicycling jerseys are popular because of their snug fit and back pockets. When purchasing a jersey, look for ones that are loaded with bright, blinding, neon logos and manufacturers' names. These loudly decorated billboards are also good for drawing unnecessary attention to yourself just before taking a mean spill while trying to hop a curb. A cotton T-shirt is a good alternative in warm weather, but when the weather turns cold, cotton becomes a chilling substitute for the jersey. Cotton retains moisture and sweat against your body, which may cause you to get the chills and ills on those cold-weather rides.

OH, THOSE CHILLY INDIANA DAYS

If the weather chooses not to cooperate on the day you've set aside for a bike ride, it's helpful to be prepared.

- **Tights or leg warmers.** These are best in temperatures below 55 degrees. Knees are sensitive and can develop all kinds of problems if they get cold. Common problems include tendinitis, bursitis, and arthritis.
- **Plenty of layers on your upper body.** When the air has a nip in it, layers of clothing will keep the chill away from your chest and help prevent the development of bronchitis. If the air is cool, a polypropylene long-sleeved shirt is best to wear against the skin beneath other layers of clothing. Polypropylene, like wool, wicks away moisture from your skin to keep your body dry. Try to avoid wearing cotton or baggy clothing when the temperature falls. Cotton, as mentioned before, holds moisture like a sponge, and baggy clothing catches cold air and swirls it around your body. Good cold-weather clothing should fit snugly against your body, but not be restrictive.
- **Wool socks.** Don't pack too many layers under those shoes, though. You may stand the chance of restricting circulation, and your feet will get real cold, real fast.
- **Thinsulate or Gortex gloves.** We may all agree that there is nothing worse than frozen feet—unless your hands are frozen. A good pair of Thinsulate or Gortex gloves should keep your hands toasty and warm.
- **Hat or helmet on cold days?** Sometimes, when the weather gets *really* cold and you *still* want to hit the trails, it's tough to stay warm. We all know that 130 percent of the body's heat escapes through the head (overactive brains, I imagine), so it's important to keep the cranium warm. Ventilated

helmets are designed to keep heads cool in the summer heat, but they do little to help keep heads warm during rides in sub-zero temperatures. Cyclists should consider wearing a hat on extremely cold days. Polypropylene Skullcaps are great head and ear warmers that snugly fit over your head beneath the helmet. Head protection is not lost. Another option is a helmet cover that covers those ventilating gaps and helps keep the body heat in. These do not, however, keep your ears warm. Some cyclists will opt for a simple knit cycling cap sans the helmet, but these have never been shown to be very good cranium protectors.

All of this clothing can be found at your local bike store, where the staff should be happy to help fit you into the seasons of the year.

TO HAVE OR NOT TO HAVE...
(Other Very Useful Items)

Though mountain biking is relatively new to the cycling scene, there is no shortage of items for you and your bike to make riding better, safer, and easier. I have rummaged through the unending lists and separated the gadgets from the good stuff, coming up with what I believe are items certain to make mountain bike riding easier and more enjoyable.

- **TIRES.** Buying yourself a good pair of knobby tires is the quickest way to enhance the off-road handling capabilities of your bike. There are many types of mountain bike tires on the market. Some are made exclusively for very rugged off-road terrain. These big-knobbed, soft rubber tires virtually stick to the ground with unforgiving traction, but tend to deteriorate quickly on pavement. There are other tires made exclusively for the road. These are called "slicks" and have no tread at all. For the average cyclist, though, a good tire somewhere in the middle of these two extremes should do the trick.

- **TOE CLIPS or CLIPLESS PEDALS.** With these, you will ride with more power. Toe clips attach to your pedals and strap your feet firmly in place, allowing you to exert pressure on the pedals on both the downstroke and the upstroke. They will increase your pedaling efficiency by 30 percent to 50 percent. Clipless pedals, which liberate your feet from the traditional straps and clips, have made toe clips virtually obsolete. Like ski bindings, they attach your shoe directly to the pedal. They are, however, much more expensive than toe clips.

- **BAR ENDS.** These great clamp-on additions to your original straight bar will provide more leverage, an excellent grip for climbing, and a more natural position for your hands. Be aware, however, of the bar end's propensity for hooking trees on fast descents, sending you, the cyclist, airborne.

- **FANNY PACK.** These bags are ideal for carrying keys, extra food, guidebooks, tools, spare tubes, and a cellular phone, in case you need to call for help.

- **SUSPENSION FORKS.** For the more serious off-roaders who want nothing to impede their speed on the trails, investing in a pair of suspension forks is a good idea. Like tires, there are plenty of brands to choose from, and they all do the same thing—absorb the brutal beatings of a rough trail. The cost of these forks, however, is sometimes more brutal than the trail itself.

- **BIKE COMPUTERS.** These are fun gadgets to own and are much less expensive than in years past. They have such features as trip distance, speedometer, odometer, time of day, altitude, alarm, average speed, maximum speed, heart rate, global satellite positioning, etc. Bike computers will come in handy when following these maps or to know just how far you've ridden in the wrong direction.

TYPES OF OFF-ROAD TERRAIN

Before roughing it off road, we may first have to ride the pavement to get to our destination. Please, don't be dismayed. Some of the country's best rides are on the road. Once we get past these smooth-surfaced pathways, though, adventures in dirt await us.

- **RAILS-TO-TRAILS.** Abandoned rail lines are converted into usable public resources for exercising, commuting, or just enjoying nature. Old rails and ties are torn up and a trail, paved or unpaved, is laid along the existing corridor. This completes the cycle from ancient Indian trading routes to railroad corridors and back again to hiking and cycling trails.

- **UNPAVED ROADS.** These are typically found in rural areas and are most often public roads. Be careful when exploring, though, not to ride on someone's unpaved private drive.

- **FOREST ROADS.** These dirt and gravel roads are used primarily as access to forest land and are kept in good condition. They are almost always open to public use.

- **SINGLETRACK.** Singletrack can be the most fun on a mountain bike. These trails, with only one track to follow, are often narrow, challenging pathways through the woods. Remember to make sure these trails are open before zipping into the woods. (At the time of this printing, all trails and roads in this guidebook were open to mountain bikes.)

- **OPEN LAND.** Unless there is a marked trail through a field or open space, you should not plan to ride here. Once one person cuts his or her wheels through a field or meadow, many more are sure to follow, causing irreparable damage to the landscape. "Human tracks are like cancer cells; they spread very quickly."

TECHNIQUES TO SHARPEN YOUR SKILLS

Many of us see ourselves as pure athletes—blessed with power, strength, and endless endurance. However, it may be those with finesse, balance, agility, and grace that get around most quickly on a mountain bike. Although power, strength, and endurance do have their places in mountain biking, these elements don't necessarily form the framework for a champion mountain biker.

The bike should become an extension of your body. Slight shifts in your hips or knees can have remarkable results. Experienced bike handlers seem to flash down technical descents, dashing over obstacles in a smooth and graceful effort as if pirouetting in *Swan Lake*.

Here are some tips and techniques to help you connect with your bike and float gracefully over the dirt.

Braking

Using your brakes requires using your head, especially when descending. This doesn't mean using your head as a stopping block, but rather to think intelligently. Use your best judgment in terms of how much or how little to squeeze those brake levers.

The more weight a tire is carrying, the more braking power it has. When you're going downhill, your front wheel carries more weight than the rear. Braking with the front brake will help keep you in control without going into a skid. Be careful, though, not to overdo it with the front brakes and accidentally toss yourself over the handlebars! And don't neglect your rear brake! When descending, shift your weight back over the rear wheel, thus increasing your rear braking power as well. This will balance the power of both brakes and give you maximum control.

Good riders learn just how much of their weight to shift over each wheel and how to apply just enough braking power to each brake, so not to "endo" over the handlebars or skid down a trail.

GOING UPHILL—Climbing Those Treacherous Hills

- **Shift into a low gear (push the thumb shifter away from you).** Before shifting, be sure to ease up on your pedaling so there is not too much pressure on the chain. Find the gear best for you that matches the terrain and steepness of each climb.
- **Stay seated.** Standing out of the saddle is often helpful when climbing

steep hills with a road bike, but you may find that on dirt, standing may cause your rear tire to lose its grip and spin out. Climbing requires traction. Stay seated as long as you can, and keep the rear tire digging into the ground. Ascending skyward may prove to be much easier *in* the saddle.

- **Lean forward.** On very steep hills, the front end may feel unweighted and suddenly pop up. Slide forward on the saddle and lean over the handlebars. This will add more weight to the front wheel and should keep you grounded.
- **Keep pedaling.** On rocky climbs, be sure to keep the pressure on, and don't let up on those pedals! The slower you go through rough trail sections, the harder you will work.

GOING DOWNHILL—
The Real Reason We Get Up in the Morning

- **Shift into the big chainring.** Shifting into the big ring before a bumpy descent will help keep the chain from bouncing off. And should you crash or disengage your leg from the pedal, the chain will cover the teeth of the big ring so they don't bite into your leg.
- **Relax.** Stay loose on the bike, and don't lock your elbows or clench your grip. Your elbows need to bend with the bumps and absorb the shock, while your hands should have a firm but controlled grip on the bars to keep things steady. Steer with your body, allowing your shoulders to guide you through each turn and around each obstacle.
- **Don't oversteer or lose control.** Mountain biking is much like downhill skiing, since you must shift your weight from side to side down narrow, bumpy descents. Your bike will have the tendency to track in the direction you look and follow the slight shifts and leans of your body. You should not think so much about steering, but rather in what direction you wish to go.
- **Rise above the saddle.** When racing down bumpy, technical descents, you should not be sitting on the saddle, but standing on the pedals, allowing your legs and knees to absorb the rocky trail instead of your rear.
- **Drop your saddle.** For steep, technical descents, you may want to drop your saddle three or four inches. This lowers your center of gravity, giving you much more room to bounce around.
- **Keep your pedals parallel to the ground.** The front pedal should be slightly higher so that it doesn't catch on small rocks or logs.
- **Stay focused.** Many descents require your utmost concentration and focus just to reach the bottom. You must notice every groove, every root, every rock, every hole, every bump. You, the bike, and the trail should all become one as you seek singletrack nirvana on your way down the mountain. But if your thoughts wander, however, then so may your bike, and you may instead become one with the trees!

WATCH OUT!

Back-road Obstacles

- **LOGS**. When you want to hop a log, throw your body back, yank up on the handlebars, and pedal forward in one swift motion. This clears the front end of the bike. Then quickly scoot forward and pedal the rear wheel up and over. Keep the forward momentum until you've cleared the log, and by all means, don't hit the brakes, or you may do some interesting acrobatic maneuvers!

- **ROCKS**. Worse than highway potholes! Stay relaxed, let your elbows and knees absorb the shock, and always continue applying power to your pedals. Staying seated will keep the rear wheel weighted to prevent slipping, and a light front end will help you to respond quickly to each new obstacle. The slower you go, the more time your tires will have to get caught between the grooves.

- **WATER**. Before crossing a stream or puddle, be sure to first check the depth and bottom surface. There may be an unseen hole or large rock hidden under the water that could wash you up if you're not careful. After you're sure all is safe, hit the water at a good speed, pedal steadily, and allow the bike to steer you through. Once you're across, tap the breaks to squeegee the water off the rims.

- **LEAVES**. Be careful of wet leaves. These may look pretty, but a trail covered with leaves may cause your wheels to slip out from under you. Leaves are not nearly as unpredictable and dangerous as ice, but they do warrant your attention on a rainy day.

- **MUD**. If you must ride through mud, hit it head on and keep pedaling. You want to part the ooze with your front wheel and get across before it swallows you up. Above all, don't leave the trail to go around the mud. This just widens the path even more and leads to increased trail erosion.

Urban Obstacles

- **CURBS** are fun to jump, but like with logs, be careful.
  - **CURBSIDE DRAINS** are typically not a problem for bikes. Just be careful not to get a wheel caught in the grate.
    - **DOGS** make great pets, but seem to have it in for bicyclists. If you think you can't outrun a dog that's chasing you, stop and walk your bike out of its territory. A loud yell to *Get!* or *Go home!* often works, as does a sharp squirt from your water bottle right between the eyes.

- **CARS** are tremendously convenient when we're in them, but dodging irate motorists in big automobiles becomes a real hazard when riding a bike. As a cyclist, you must realize most drivers aren't expecting you to be there and often wish you weren't. Stay alert and ride carefully, clearly signaling all of your intentions.
- **POTHOLES**, like grates and back-road canyons, should be avoided. Just because you're on an all-terrain bicycle doesn't mean you're indestructible. Potholes regularly damage rims, pop tires, and sometimes lift unsuspecting cyclists into a spectacular swan dive over the handlebars.

LAST-MINUTE CHECKOVER

Before a ride, it's a good idea to give your bike a once-over to make sure everything is in working order. Begin by checking the air pressure in your tires before each ride to make sure they are properly inflated. Mountain bikes require about 45 to 55 pounds per square inch of air pressure. If your tires are underinflated, there is greater likelihood that the tubes may get pinched on a bump or rock, causing the tire to flat.

Looking over your bike to make sure everything is secure and in its place is the next step. Go through the following checklist before each ride.

- **Pinch the tires to feel for proper inflation**. They should give just a little on the sides, but feel very hard on the treads. If you have a pressure gauge, use that.
- **Check your brakes**. Squeeze the rear brake and roll your bike forward. The rear tire should skid. Next, squeeze the front brake and roll your bike forward. The rear wheel should lift into the air. If this doesn't happen, then your brakes are too loose. Make sure the brake levers don't touch the handlebars when squeezed with full force.
- **Check all quick releases on your bike**. Make sure they are all securely tightened.
- **Lube up**. If your chain squeaks, apply some lubricant.

- **Check your nuts and bolts.** Check the handlebars, saddle, cranks, and pedals to make sure that each is tight and securely fastened to your bike.
- **Check your wheels.** Spin each wheel to see that they spin through the frame and between brake pads freely.
- **Have you got everything?** Make sure you have your spare tube, tire irons patch kit, frame pump, tools, food, water, and guidebook.

Liability Disclaimer

Beachway Press assumes no liability for cyclists traveling along any of the suggested routes in this book. At the time of publication, all routes shown on the following maps were open to bicycles. They were chosen for their safety, aesthetics, and pleasure, and are deemed acceptable and accommodating to bicyclists. Safety upon these routes, however, cannot be guaranteed. Cyclists must assume their own responsibility when riding these routes and understand that with an activity such as mountain bike riding, there may be unforeseen risks and dangers.

The Maps

I don't want anyone, by any means, to feel restricted to just these roads and trails that I have mapped. I hope you will have the same adventurous spirit and use these maps as a platform to dive into Indiana's backcountry, discovering new routes for yourself. One of the best ways to begin this is to simply turn the map upside down and ride the course in reverse. The change in perspective is fantastic and the ride should feel quite different. With this in mind, it will be like getting two distinctly different rides on each map.

For your own purposes, you may wish to copy the directions for the course onto a small sheet to help you while riding, or photocopy the map and cue sheet to take with you. These pages can be carried with you easily using the BarMap® or BarMap OTG® (note description on last page), or can simply be folded into a bike bag or stuffed into a jersey pocket. Please remember to slow or even stop when you want to read the map.

After a short introduction, there is a profile map of each route followed by a cue sheet, which provides detailed directions and information about each ride.

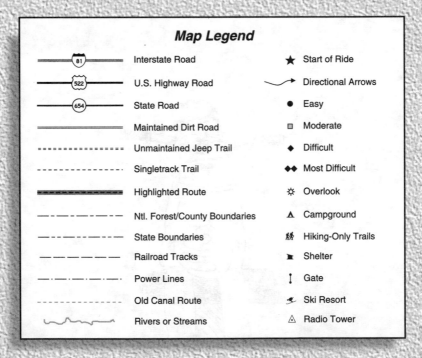

Map Legend

——81—— Interstate Road	★ Start of Ride
——522—— U.S. Highway Road	⌐→ Directional Arrows
——654—— State Road	● Easy
———— Maintained Dirt Road	▢ Moderate
·············· Unmaintained Jeep Trail	◆ Difficult
- - - - - - Singletrack Trail	◆◆ Most Difficult
▬▬▬▬ Highlighted Route	☼ Overlook
—— —— —— Ntl. Forest/County Boundaries	▲ Campground
— — — — State Boundaries	林 Hiking-Only Trails
— — — — Railroad Tracks	⊮ Shelter
—·—·—·— Power Lines	I Gate
- - - - - - Old Canal Route	⚞ Ski Resort
∿∿∿ Rivers or Streams	△ Radio Tower

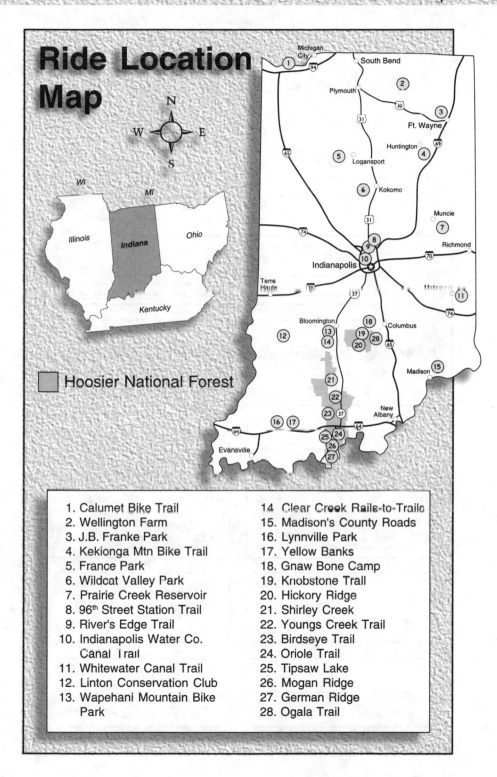

Ride Location Map

N
W · E
S

WI
MI
Illinois
Indiana
Ohio
Kentucky

Michigan City
South Bend
Plymouth
Ft. Wayne
Huntington
Logansport
Kokomo
Muncie
Richmond
Indianapolis
Terre Haute
Bloomington
Columbus
Madison
New Albany
Evansville

☐ Hoosier National Forest

1. Calumet Bike Trail
2. Wellington Farm
3. J.B. Franke Park
4. Kekionga Mtn Bike Trail
5. France Park
6. Wildcat Valley Park
7. Prairie Creek Reservoir
8. 96th Street Station Trail
9. River's Edge Trail
10. Indianapolis Water Co. Canal Trail
11. Whitewater Canal Trail
12. Linton Conservation Club
13. Wapehani Mountain Bike Park

14. Clear Creek Rails-to-Trails
15. Madison's County Roads
16. Lynnville Park
17. Yellow Banks
18. Gnaw Bone Camp
19. Knobstone Trail
20. Hickory Ridge
21. Shirley Creek
22. Youngs Creek Trail
23. Birdseye Trail
24. Oriole Trail
25. Tipsaw Lake
26. Mogan Ridge
27. German Ridge
28. Ogala Trail

Courses at a Glance

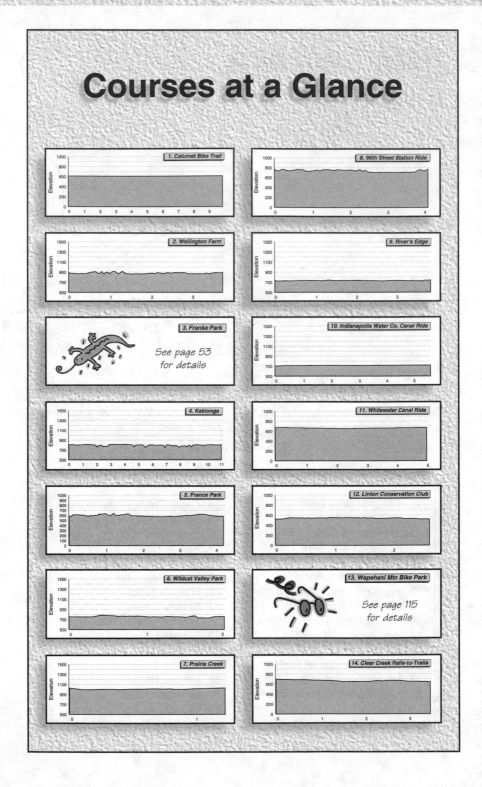

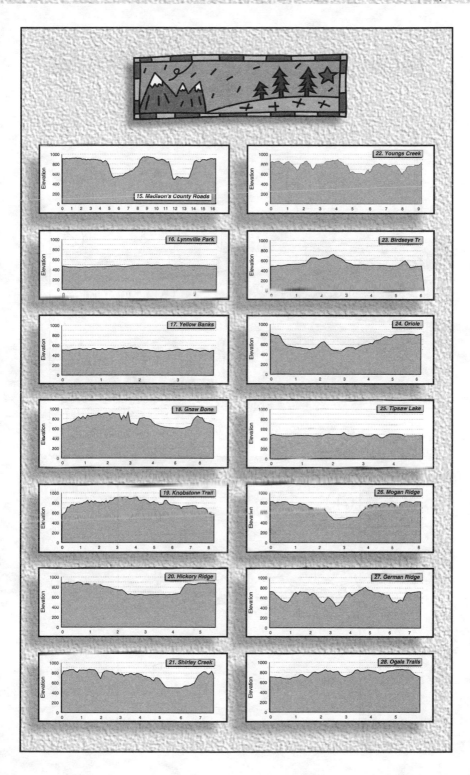

How To Use These Maps

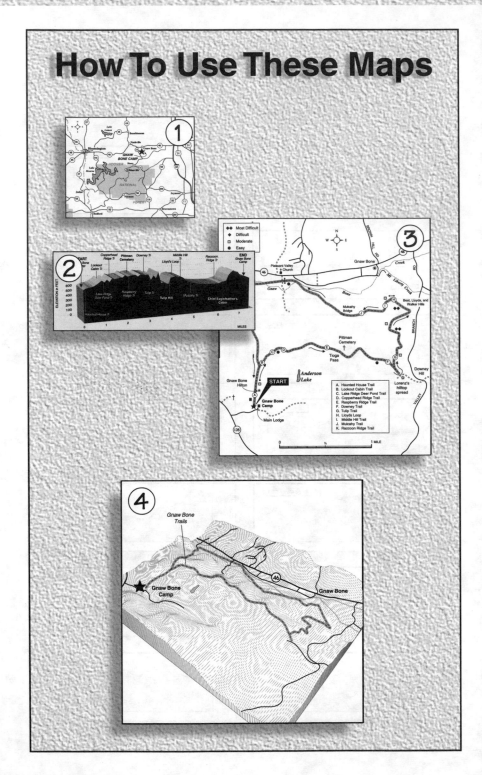

(1) Location Map. This map helps you find your way to the start of each ride from the nearest sizeable town or city. Coupled with the detailed directions at the beginning of the cue, this map should visually lead you to where you need to be to hit the trails.

(2) 3D Profile Map. This three-dimensional profile gives you a cross-sectional look at the ride's ups and downs. Elevation is labeled on the left, mileage is indicated on the bottom, towns and points of interest are shown above the map in **bold**. Road and trail names, also shown above the map, are labeled in *italics*.

(3) Road Map. This is your primary guide to each ride. It shows all of the accessible roads and trails, points of interest, water, towns, landmarks, and geographical features. It also distinguishes trails from roads and paved roads from unpaved roads. The selected route is highlighted, and directional arrows point the way.

(4) 3D Surface Area Map. This three-dimensional look at the earth's surface within the area of the selected ride gives you an accurate representation of the surrounding topography and landscape. The map has been rotated for the best view and includes important roads and trails as well as distinguishable features for points of reference.

Ride Information Board. This is a small bulletin board with important information concerning each ride.

- The **Trail Maintenance Hotline** is the direct number for the local land managers in charge of all the trails within the selected ride. Use this hotline right away if there is ever a problem with trail erosion, damage, or misuse.
- **Cost.** What money, if any, you may need to carry with you for park entrance fees or tolls.
- **Schedule.** This tells you what time trails open and close, and if they are on private or park land.
- **Maps.** This is a list of other maps to supplement the maps in this book. They are listed in order from most detailed to most general.

1

Calumet Bike Trail

Ride Specs

Start: Dune Acres Road parking

Length: 9.9 miles one way

Rating: Easy

Terrain: Flat; sand & gravel surface

Riding Time: 2½ hours

Other Uses: Camping, hiking, hanging out at the beach

More than 100 years ago, adventure journalist Thomas B. Stephens pedaled along the northern edge of the state on his high-wheeler bicycle during his successful quest to ride around the world. On a portion of his 2,500-mile jaunt, Stephens rode from Chicago to South Bend, at one point actually riding along the shore of Lake Michigan on the Calumet Trail.

While riding along that same trail, one can't help but wonder how the sights have changed since Stephen's trek. And on summer days in the sweltering heat, one can't help feel the same discomforts as Stephens might have felt.

After 18 miles of good riding and tough trundling through deep sand, Stephens pedaled over the Indiana state line. For the first 35 miles he rode around the edge of Lake Michigan. Finding the wagon roads next to impossible, he pedaled around the hard, wet sand near the water's edge.

From Steven's book, *Around the World on a Bicycle*, he recalls the Hoosier state — "This place is enough to give one the yellow-edged blues: nothing but swamps, sand, sad-eyed turtles, and ruthless, relentless mosquitoes. At Chesterton the roads improve, but still enough sand remains to break the force of headers, which, notwithstanding my long experience on the road, I still manage to execute with undesirable frequency."

Today the trail is in a dilapidated state and possibly resembles what Stephens crossed during his journey. The route's neglected state is probably what led many officials to redirect my calls before admitting the trail was officially open. And with good reason. At one point, underneath the gravel, sand, and grassy remains, the path appears to have once been paved and

---

Getting There

☞ **From Michigan City** – Take **Hwy 12 west** approximately 12 miles to **Dune Acres Road**. Turn **right** on **Dune Acres Road** and travel 0.2 miles to the **parking area** on the **left**.

Author looking smug atop Mt. Baldy after shouldering his bike to the dune's summit.

maintained. In its present state it looks as if a crew simply bushhogs the weeds to clear a path.

As road cyclists witness the demise of Calumet Trail, though, mountain bikers rejoice and claim the route as their own. Less maintenance means less traffic, which offers the possibility of riding the entire straight and flat corridor without passing a single cyclist.

In the height of summer, the trail is surrounded by shoulder-high wildflowers. Bordering the wildflowers to the north is a thick hardwood forest that acts as a breaker from the lake's winds.

A completely different landscape rewards cyclists at the ride's completion. Shoulder your bike and climb Mt. Baldy. The unobstructed view from atop this mountain dune is surreal and takes your imagination from Midwestern farmland to the ocean coast of your choice.

A constant breeze whispers through the dune grass as waves roll against the shore. This breeze keeps Mt. Baldy and the other dunes alive. The stiff lake wind lifts sand particles and deposits them on the ever-moving dunes, while on the back side of the dunes, the sand blowing over the top

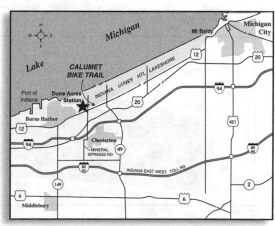

looks as if the dune is smoking.

The Indiana Dunes National Lakeshore is also noted for having one of the few singing beaches in the world. Of course, the dunes don't just sing for anyone; they must be prompted. To start the chorus, walk near the water's edge with your bare feet. The compression of the quartz crystals, moisture, and friction from your feet creates a clear ringing sound.

The work of the Ice Age can also be spotted on the dunes. But instead of crumpling the landscape like the glaciers did to the southern

Mt. Baldy

One of the largest dunes on the southern shore of Lake Michigan, it is 123 feet tall and is advancing inland at a rate of 4 to 5 feet per year. Northwest winds move Mt. Baldy inland, slowly burying the forest just south of the dune. Winds pick up the sand grains from the beach and blow them inland. The sand grains roll and bounce along in a process referred to as "saltation." As the wind speed increases, the sand is picked up and carried. Viewed from a distance, the sand blowing off the top of Mt. Baldy appears as wisps of smoke, thus the term "smoking dune."— *Department of Natural Resources, Indiana Dunes National Lakeshore.*

third of the state, the remnants are a multitude of plants from many different environments. Arctic bearberry bushes can be found next to desert-like prickly pear cactus, and dogwoods from southern latitudes can be found growing in close proximity to northern jack pines.

Walking along the shore, looking north, Lake Michigan appears endless. To the west lies a reminder of the dunes proximity to Chicago. On clear days, the tops of skyscrapers in the "City of Broad Shoulders" can be seen over the lake's western horizon.

Take in the sites along the shore, then move inward to the bogs. Your options include hiking along Cowles Bog Trail, bird-watching on the Island Marsh Trail, searching for the sad-eyed turtles Thomas Stephens wrote about, or visiting the nature center near Mt. Tom.

After a full day of riding, beach combing, bird-watching, and ecological study, mosey on over to the Dunewood Campground and pitch your tent for the night. The dunes hold something for everyone.

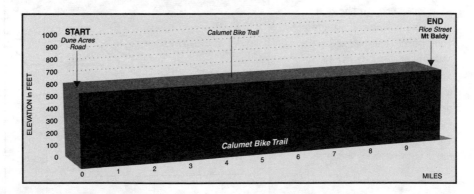

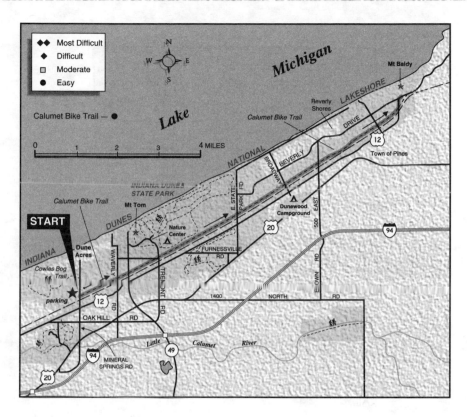

MILES   DIRECTIONS

0.0   **START** at **Dune Acres Road Parking Area.** Find the trailhead east of the parking area, just across the street.

0.5   CALUMET TRAIL crosses a gravel driveway

1.1   **CALUMET TRAIL** crosses **Waverly Road.**

1.5   Arrive at a **trail intersection.** Continue **straight** on the CALUMET TRAIL, passing the **Dune Park Railroad Station** on the right.

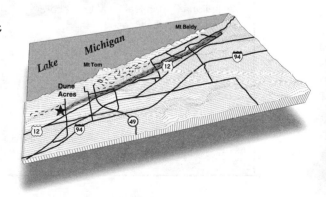

2.1   **CALUMET TRAIL** crosses a gravel driveway.

2.2   CALUMET TRAIL crosses **Tremont Road**.

4.5   CALUMET TRAIL crosses **East State Park Road**.

4.6   Pass a trail heading off to the left. Continue **straight** on the
       CALUMET TRAIL.

5.9   CALUMET TRAIL intersects with **Broadway**. Turn **left** on **Broad-
       way**, then take a quick **right** into a **gravel parking** lot to the
       trailhead.

7.5   Pass a trail on the right. Continue **straight** on the CALUMET
       TRAIL.

7.6   Turn **right** on the **singletrack trail**. Follow the trail along the
       railroad tracks. Cyclists cannot go straight along Calumet Trail
       proper. **Calumet Trail** is washed out here and cyclists must go
       around to the tracks, then back down to the trail.

Ride Information

Trail Maintenance Hotline:

Indiana Dunes National Lakeshore	(219) 926-7561
Indiana Dunes State Park	(219) 926-1952
Emergencies: Bailly Ranger Station	1-800-727-5847

Schedule:

    Calumet Trail open year-round

    Visitor Center open daily except January 1, Thanksgiving, and
        December 25

Maps:

    USGS maps: Dune Acres, IN; Michigan City West, IN

    Indiana Dunes Official Map and Guide

7.7   Take the **singletrack trail** off the tracks and back to CALUMET TRAIL.

8.1   CALUMET TRAIL crosses an unmarked gravel road.

8.7   CALUMET TRAIL crosses **Central Avenue.**

8.8   CALUMET TRAIL crosses an unmarked dirt road.

9.1   CALUMET TRAIL crosses an unmarked paved road. An electrical cooling tower that looks like a nuclear power plant comes into view. We can only hope that Homer Simpson is not at the controls!

9.3   CALUMET TRAIL ends at **Hwy 12.** Turn **left** on **Hwy 12.**

9.7   Turn **left** on **Rice Street.** The road is marked by the **"Indiana Dunes National Lakeshore/Mt. Baldy"** sign.

9.9   **Rice Street** ends at the **Mt. Baldy** parking area and trailhead. Restrooms are available here.

2 Wellington Farm Mtn Bike Trail

Ride Specs

Start: Four wooden posts in the parking area

Length: 3.7 miles

Rating: Difficult

Terrain: Twisting singletrack

Riding Time: 30 minutes – 1 hour

Other Uses: Hiking

More than 10,000 years ago, glaciers cleared the topographic slate clean and left little landscape in what is now northern Indiana for mountain bikers to enjoy. Today the majority of this area is farmland. Thus, pursuit of challenging legal trails is a never-ending battle.

However, the glaciers did leave behind a few hilly moraines and kettle holes for mountain bikers to work with in this area of northeastern Indiana. These holes filled with water long ago and formed a condensed cluster of lakes, the largest being Lake Wawasee.

Spanning 2,618 acres, Lake Wawasee is Indiana's largest natural lake. Years ago the body of water was named Turkey Lake, but was later renamed after Miami Chief Wau-wa-aus-see. Lake Wawasee is now surrounded by hotels, camps, cottages, boat liveries, riding stables, golf courses, and a repertory theater.

Traditionally, the lake has been a summer playground. But with the addition of many winter sports to the area, there is year-round activity in town. With the addition of a mountain bike loop at Wellington Farm, mountain biking can also be added to the list of recreational activities.

Granted, this area is a topographic challenge, but there are just enough features on the 96-acre Wellington Farm for a solid trail system. That's exactly what Jim Wellington and his uncle John Wellington did. John owned the

Getting There

☞ **From Ft. Wayne** – Take **Hwy 30 west** approximately 27 miles to **Hwy 13**. Take **Hwy 13 north** approximately 17 miles to **Syracuse**. From **downtown Syracuse**, continue **north** on **Hwy 13** approximately 1 mile. Take the **first left** past **County Line Road South** and the guardrail. If you drive past **Commodore Homes** or **Hwy 6**, you have driven too far. Follow the driveway past the house and barn. **Park** in the **open area** past the **four posts** sticking out of the ground on the right.

"Exiting" the trail at Wellington Farm.

acreage north of Syracuse, and Jim had the gumption to dub the trails.

While most trail construction projects occur during the winter when thickets and thorns are most vulnerable, Jim decided to complete the work during summertime. In the sweltering heat and humidity, the thorny briars' tentacles sprawl across the ground. Undaunted, Jim and a few friends tackled the project with chainsaws and axes. Jim crawled under the briar bushes and cut through their center. The bush would fall on top of him, he'd climb out, then move on to the next bush.

The biggest physical challenges were the briars, thickets, and grapevines that flourished on the land. An even larger obstacle, though, was the fact that there was only one major hill on the whole property. Jim capitalized on this one hill, as the trail climbs and descends it six times.

After six months, a four-mile course was laid out, and plans for another 1.5 miles of trail are in the works. One year later, the Wellingtons pulled off a successful mountain bike race, earning the accolades of cyclists across the state. To the trail's benefit, cyclists packed down the muddy trail and cleared out the freshly cut grass during the race, which helped form the course.

The trails of Wellington Farm are well laid out and seem to have little environmental impact. This short-course system winds through oak, hickory, redbud, and dogwood trees, enhancing the area as opposed to disrupting it. Wildlife have taken to the area's newest

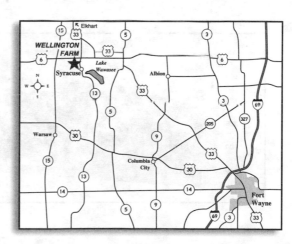

arrival as well, and appear to co-exist quite nicely. Barn owls, deer, wild turkey, and waterfowl can all be spotted on the property.

Through the wildflowers...

This single-loop trail squeezes in twists and turns, climbs and descents, and high-speed field crossings through some very challenging singletrack without damaging the field and wooded areas.

This course is not beginner friendly by any means, however. In the condensed sections, there are more switchbacks than the Alpe d'Huez stage of the Tour de France. From each winding section there is a short, straight section that barely allows one to catch his breath. And the climbs, though limited to one hill, require strong legs to summit.

As far as checking in, there is no registration process. Simply drive in and ride the trails. The owner, however, requests that all cyclists stay on the Wellington property — *the house and barn are not Wellington property.* As of yet, folks residing in the house don't seem to mind the cyclists. The main drive at this house leads back to the parking area, but John prefers cyclists use the field entrance just past County Line Road South and the guardrail.

MILES   DIRECTIONS

0.0   **START** at the **four posts** and follow the trail toward the treeline, away from Hwy 13.

0.1   The trail leaves the field and bends into the trees. This is the first switchback section.

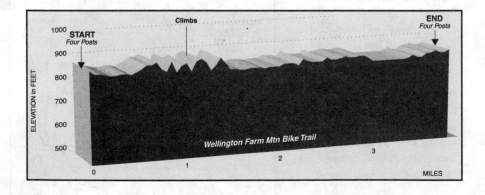

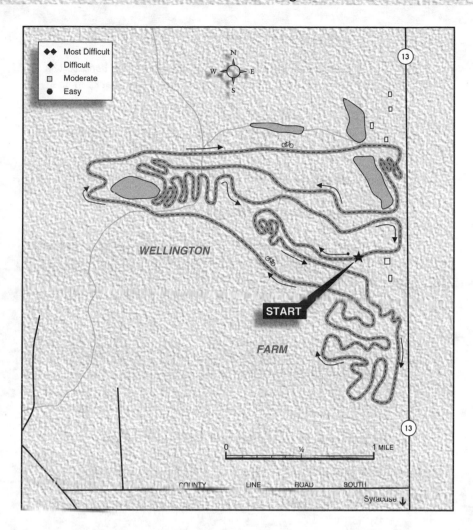

0.4   A trail goes off to the left. Continue **straight** on the **main trail**. The trail on the left leads back to the parking area.

0.5   The trail splits. Follow the singletrack split to the **right** and follow the perimeter of the field.

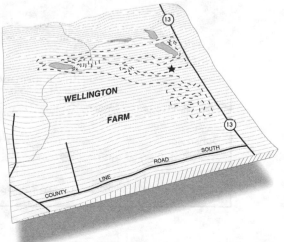

0.55   The trail leads back into the woods.

0.7   A trail goes off to the left. Follow the **main trail** and bend to the **right**. There are many climbs, descents, and switchbacks in this section.

1.3   The trail follows the low-point on the topo before turning back and climbing into the woods.

1.7   Pass a **swamp** on the left.

2.1   The trail splits. Take the **left split**.

2.2   The singletrack dumps out into a field. It follows the perimeter of the field and is across from the parking area.

2.4   Pass between **two ponds**. Now near **Hwy 13**. A few switchbacks are in this section.

2.6   The trail dumps out into the field.

2.9   The trail crosses a **fenceline** and winds through some shrubs.

3.2   The trail dumps back out to the field and bends to the **right**.

3.3   The trail splits. Take the **left split** and cross the field.

3.4   The trail bends to the **right** and runs parallel to **Hwy 13**.

3.7   Pass the **four poles** sticking out of the ground to complete the loop.

Ride Information

Trail Maintenance Hotline:
    John Wellington   (219) 457-2020
Schedule:
    Open dawn to dusk, year-round
Maps:
    USGS maps: Milford, IN; Lake Wawasee, IN

3 J.B. Franke Park

Ride Specs

Start: Nature Center

Length: 15-miles of rideable trails

Rating: Moderate

Terrain: Rolling, wooded singletrack

Riding Time: 30 minutes – 1½ hours

Other Uses: Hiking, soap box derby racing, BMX racing, zoo, softball, football

As Indiana's second-largest city, Fort Wayne's roots can be traced to when it was once a prime military post. This garrison served as a trading and military center to the Miami, Iroquois, French, English, and finally the Americans. This strategic post placement sits at the intersection of three rivers: the St. Joseph, the St. Marys, and the Maumee, each of which is connected to the Great Lakes and the Mississippi River.

So it came as no surprise then, as riverboat commerce and canal popularity increased, that Fort Wayne grew to become Indiana's fifth largest city. When river travel was replaced by the railroad, Fort Wayne smartly replaced its canals with rails and continued to grow.

This prosperous city attracted many famous early Americans. Thomas Edison arrived in town and worked the railroad nearly six months. Not to be outdone, his-soon-to-be-competitor, George Westinghouse, came to Fort Wayne to test his first air brake.

John Chapman, another early American icon, is buried within the city limits. Chapman, better known as "Johnny Appleseed," traveled the country wearing his trademark hat, bare feet, and flour sack full of seeds, planting apple trees and other fruits and vegetables along the way. Chapman has since risen to legendary lore rivaling John Henry and Paul Bunyan.

John B. Franke may not have planted apple trees, but he was owner of the Perfection Biscuit Company, and he too has left his mark on the city. Franke Park holds an estimated 15 miles of trails, a 13-acre pond, nature center, BMX course, playgrounds, picnic shelters, baseball diamonds, football field, soap

---

Getting There

☞ **From the north side of Fort Wayne** – From **I-69** on the north side of Fort Wayne, take **Goshen Road south** to **Sherman Blvd**. Turn **left** on **Sherman Blvd**. Follow **Sherman Blvd**. 0.4 miles, then turn **left** into **Franke Park's main entrance**. Turn **left** at the first available opportunity and follow the **park road** to the **Nature Center**.

box derby track, the Foellinger Theatre, and the Fort Wayne Children's Zoo.

The zoo, open from late April to late October, has over 1,000 animals in its 40-acre park. A visit to the zoo is a great reward for completing a challenging singletrack ride. You could also enjoy a picnic lunch or just rest beneath one of the plentiful shade trees.

The trails of this 280-acre park are intertwining, challenging, twisting, and predominantly singletrack. This system offers an inner-city getaway for urban cyclists without the long drive to make such an escape. While these trails were a challenge to map, an even bigger challenge would be to ride the same loop twice. The benefit of having such a condensed trail system, though, is that it is possible to get a great workout without fear of getting lost.

A couple of trail highlights include the two race courses at the back of the park. Take a lap around the BMX track and test your skills on the camelback hills and the banked, hairpin turns. Climb the hill to the top of the soap box derby track, which is also used as a toboggan run in the winter, and take in the view of the park and surrounding subdivision.

For advanced cyclists, the exhilarating downhill run

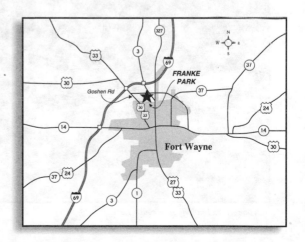

Ride Information

Trail Maintenance Hotline:
Fort Wayne Parks Dept.   (219) 427-6000
Children's Zoo   (219) 427-6800
Drive-in Theatre   1-800-727-5847

Schedule:
Franke Park: 5 a.m. - 11 p.m.
Children's Zoo: Open Mon-Sat, 9-5 p.m., Sun. & Holidays, 9-6 p.m.
    Late April to late October

Maps:
USGS map: Fort Wayne West, IN

off the backside of the soap box track definitely gets the blood pumping. A clear stretch after the hill allows cyclists to enjoy the speed before the trail twists back into the woods, causing cyclists to brake for those pesky speed barriers otherwise known as trees.

Also for advanced cyclists, the most challenging portion of the trail is just west of the soap box derby track. Behind the tree line are some challenging climbs and descents as the trail climbs up and down the hills along the creek.

Cyclists looking to improve their technical skills could create a short loop in this section. But make sure you don't wear yourself out. With so much fun condensed into such a small park, it would be a shame not to take advantage of it all.

Advanced technology at Franke Park.

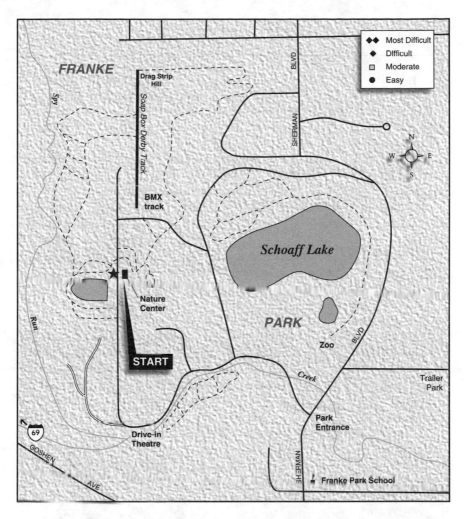

Note: Because Franke Park has so many individual trails suitable for cycling, it would be unreasonable to create a single loop. Instead, cyclists are encouraged to use the map provided and select your own routes through the park, cycling from the Nature Center to Drag Strip Hill, past Schoaff Lake toward the zoo, and everywhere in-between. For this reason, there is no profile map available.

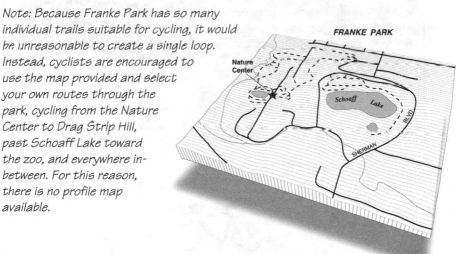

Johnny Appleseed

John Chapman was born on September 26, 1774, in Leominster, Massachusetts. In the fall of 1797, John decided to head west, hiking to Pennsylvania's Allegheny Mountains. Blue-eyed and shoeless, John carried a rifle, hatchet, and a knapsack of food and apple seeds he had gathered from the cider mills of eastern Pennsylvania.

Fighting an early squall, John wrapped his feet with cloth and descended to the town of Warren, Pennsylvania. It was here that he cleared a plot and planted his first orchard. He knew he could make a business of raising apple trees and selling its fruit to frontiersmen. This particular fruit was extremely practical, as it was used for pies, butter, cider, fermented hard cider, or eaten raw.

So every fall, John traveled east to collect free bushels of apple seeds from the cider mills. Carrying his precious cargo by horseback or canoe, John scouted for new sites farther west. Once found, the land was cleared, a fence was built, and the seeds were planted.

John spent his summers tending to his nurseries. By the time he was 40, John had orchards in Pennsylvania, Ohio, and Indiana. Before his death on March 18, 1845, John's estate had grown to 15,000 trees, 2,000 seedlings, and approximately 800 acres of land. Active to his last day, traveling barefoot and unarmed through the hostile wilderness, and giving appleseeds and fruit to pioneer children and the poor all helped perpetuate the legend of Johnny Appleseed.

Chapman walked long distances up to the day he died. If he wasn't walking, he was canoeing or riding a horse to tend to his trees. One tale even recalls Chapman riding a Cannondale duel-suspension frame down the backside of the soap box derby hill at Franke Park. Wearing a mush-pot shaped helmet, Johnny raced at high speeds pedaling with bare feet, spreading appleseeds as he went, while still leading a field of professional mountain bike racers.

Sometimes it's so difficult to separate myth from fact.

Kekionga Mtn Bike Trail 4

Ride Specs

Start: Little Turtle Gatehouse

Length: 11 miles

Rating: Easy to Moderate

Terrain: Flat; wooded singletrack

Riding Time: 2 hours

Other Uses: Camping, hiking, boating, swimming, fishing

I spell it *potatoe*, you spell it *potato*. Potato. Potatoe. What's going on here?

Why open the Kekionga Trail ride with song, you ask? And misspell potato no less? That's because the Kekionga trail that circles the Huntington Reservoir not only supplies water to the city of Huntington, but, more importantly, to the Dan Quayle Center and Museum. Built in 1992, this building houses many exhibits highlighting our 44th vice president's career. For more information, call or write the Dan Quayle Center and Museum (see Ride Information Box).

Vice-presidential satire aside, the Kekionga Trail stands out in Hoosier history not for being the closest trail to the museum, but as the first legal trail opened on state-owned property. As many cyclists know, many of the state's best trails are found in Indiana state parks. As of yet, all of these state parks, with the exception of Kekionga, are closed to mountain biking. But if all goes well along the Kekionga, much of that may change.

In the state's defense, it should be noted that mountain biking has always been permitted on state property, but only in designated areas. The irony here is that there were never any designated areas established. So after years of debate, the Indiana Bicycle Coalition, in conjunction with the Department of Natural Resources, have developed this pilot trail program at Huntington.

Both agencies will monitor trail usage, as well as the impact cyclists have on the trail. From their reports, the agencies will write the standards and policies that will govern mountain bike trail areas around the state. Cliff Johnson, the coalition's director, has taken the first step here at Huntington in helping to open

Getting There

☞ **From Fort Wayne** – Take **I-69 south** approximately 7 miles to **Hwy 24 (Exit 102)**. Take **Hwy 24 west** 18.8 miles to **Hwy 5**. Take **Hwy 5 south** approximately 1.9 miles to downtown **Huntington**. Take **Hwy 224/Hwy 5 south** 1.7 miles to **Hwy 5** split. Take **Hwy 5 south** 2.1 miles to **Little Turtle S.R.A (State Recreation Area)**.

the many great trails within Indiana's state parks.

For cyclists in northern Indiana, the Kekionga Trail is one of these great places to ride. This 11-mile loop is evenly divided between singletrack and easy-rolling grassy trails. It is a predominantly easy loop, but listed as slightly moderate for its distance and somewhat challenging singletrack on the north side of the reservoir.

One treat the trail offers is found at the reservoir's east end. County Road 200 East causeway acts as an aviary watchtower that affords an incredible view of the lake and its raptor inhabitants, without disturbing the birds' daily routines. On a typical day turkey vultures circle on rising air currents or rest on the grey branches of shoreline trees. Many great blue herons are also seen wading through shallow water, hunting for their next meal.

Continuing along the trail, cyclists come upon a series of fitness stations. If for some reason you feel that the ride is not enough of a workout, you have the option of dismounting and performing the suggested exercises.

Near the end of the loop along Highway 5, cyclists will approach the Observation Mound. Artifacts, skeletons, and other mounds have been discovered in this area. The Observation Mound stands as a preserved natural monument to the ancient Native American Adena Culture.

At the end of the trail, campsites can be found near the gate of the Little Turtle State Recreation Area. There are no showers at this campground, but clean restrooms are found near the beach area. Additional campsites are available on the other side of the reservoir.

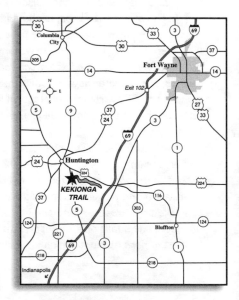

Other post-ride activities that Huntington has to offer include flying airplanes at the model airplane area, fishing, boating, and, of course, a trip to the Dan Quayle Center and Museum. Just don't make any "potatoe" cracks while you are there. The curators just don't seem to see the humor.

Overlooking Huntington Lake.

MILES   DIRECTIONS

0.0   **START** at the **Little Turtle Gatehouse**. Find the trailhead along the treeline directly west of the gatehouse.

0.1   The trail comes to a "T." Take the **left** trail.

1.0   The trail crosses a **gravel road** and the parking area for the **model plane flying area**.

1.4   The trail splits. Take the **left split**.

1.5   The trail splits. Take the **left singletrack split**. The right split leads to a field.

1.55   The trail goes through a ditch then comes to a "T." Take the **right** trail.

1.6   The trail crosses a **paved road**. Continue **straight** on the trail.

1.7   The trail bends then comes to a "T." Take the **left** trail.

2.0   The trail crosses a **creek**.

2.1   Arrive at an off-center **trail intersection**. Continue **"straight"** through the intersection.

2.3   The trail comes to a "T" at the edge of a field. Take the **left** trail.

2.31   Turn **left** on the "Scout Trail".

2.5   The trail comes to a "T." Take the **left** trail.

2.6   The trail merges into a larger trail. Continue **straight**.

2.7   Follow the trail that heads off to the **left**.

2.8   The trail comes to a "T" at an open field. Take the **left** trail.

3.0   Take the **right trail**, following the trail sign.

3.1   The trail splits. Take the **left split** following the trail sign.

3.6   The trail comes to a "T." Take the **left trail** and roll past the gate.
       The trail then crosses a **gravel road**.

4.0   Arrive at a **trail intersection**. Continue **straight** on the trail.

4.1   Arrive at a **trail intersection**. Continue **straight** on the trail.

4.15   Pass a trail on the right, then arrive at a **trail intersection**. Take
       the **left** trail. Immediately pass a trail to the left. Continue
       straight.

4.2   Come to an open area with a **pond** on the right. Roll across the
       open area to a **gravel road**. Follow the gravel road around to the
       split and take the **right split**, following the **perimeter of the pond**.

4.4   The trail fades at the base of the hill. Follow the left side of the hill
       to **County Road 200 East**.

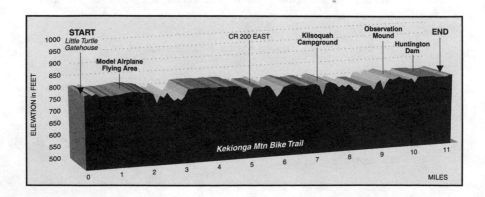

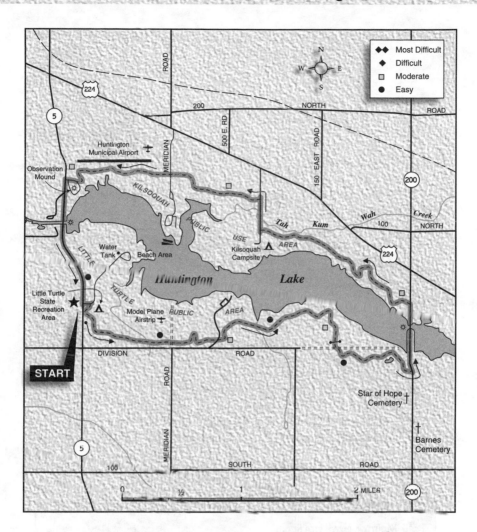

4.5 Arrive at **County Road 200 East**. Turn **left** and cross the **cause-way**.

5.1 Turn **left** off **County Road 200 East** onto a **grassy trail**.

5.3 The main trail bends to the left. There is a singletrack path to the right, but stay on the main trail.

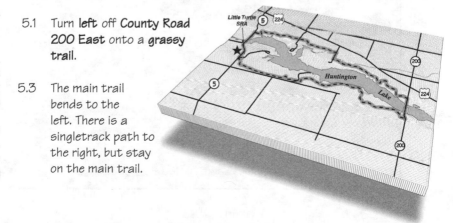

5.7   The trail goes off to the right. Continue **straight** on the main trail.

5.8   The trail splits. Take the **left split**.

5.9   The trail splits. Take the **right split**.

6.4   The trail splits. Take the **left split** and cross a **wooden bridge**.

6.5   The trail splits. Take the **left split** and cross another **wooden bridge**.

6.6   The trail splits. Take the **right split**. The left split leads to the **Kilsoquah camping area**.

6.9   The trail crosses a **wooden bridge**. Arrive at a **trail intersection**. Continue **straight** on the singletrack.

7.3   The trail crosses a **paved road** that leads to the **Kilsoquah campground**. Take a **right** on the PAVED ROAD.

7.6   Turn **left** onto singletrack at the trailhead.

8.7   The trail intersects with **Meridian Road** which leads to the **Kilsoquah boat ramp**. Continue **straight** on the trail.

9.3   The trail splits. Take the **main trail** split to the **left**.

Ride Information

Trail Maintenance Hotline:
Indiana Bicycle Coalition   (317) 327-8356
    3649 Cold Springs Rd   1-800-920-1405
    Indianapolis, IN 46222
Other Things To Do:
Dan Quayle Center and Museum   (219) 356-6356
    815 Warren Street
    P.O. Box 856
    Huntington, IN 46750-0856
Trail Schedule:
    Open dawn to dusk, year-round
Maps:
    USGS maps: Majenica, IN
    Kekionga Trail Map available at Little Turtle Campground

9.6   The trail ends at the **Observation Mound Road**. Turn **right** on this road.

9.7   Turn **left** on **Hwy 5**. Cross the **Huntington Reservoir Dam**.

10.8   Pass the **Huntington Reservoir Headquarters** on the left. Cut diagonally across the grassy field toward the **gatehouse** and the trailhead.

11.0   Ride complete. A potato would taste good right about now!

5

France Park

Ride Specs

Start: Parking lot above waterfalls

Length: 4.2 miles of 15-mile system

Rating: Moderate

Terrain: Limestone, gravel

Riding Time: 30 minutes – 2 hours

Other Uses: Hiking, horseback, camping, scuba diving, snowmobiling

Logansport, nicknamed "The Bridge City" for its numerous structures straddling the Eel and Wabash Rivers, hosts one of northern Indiana's larger mountain bike trail systems.

The primarily singletrack trails of France Park wind through land once occupied by the Miami and Potawatomi people. The Erie Canal also edges one of the trails—a faint reminder of the historical importance placed on water travel.

Local mountain biker Brent Mullen was my guide for the day, leading me through the different loops that wind around quarries, through woods, and past patches of stinging nettles. He even managed to shed some positive light on the abundance of stinging nettles, explaining how to boil their leaves to make a delicious tea (see sidebar on page 67).

France Park was established in 1967. In addition to mountain biking, the park provides many family activities, including numerous campsites, a scenic picnic area at the base of the falls, a well-groomed beachfront, and even a putt-putt golf course.

While riding on the trail, stop to savor the view atop the ridge of the swimming quarry. Look into the pearly green water and try to spot one of the many spoonbilled paddlefish snaking around just below the surface. These algae eaters were imported from Missouri and stocked at a cost of $500. Locals claim some grow as long as seven feet! You may also spot moving fountains of air bubbles dotting the water's surface. These are schools of scuba divers viewing the remains of a bus, truck, and train wheels that have been laid to rest at the bottom of the pit.

Getting There

☞ **From Lafayette** – Take **Hwy 25 north** approximately 38 miles to **Logansport**. Take **Hwy 35 north** approximately 1 mile to **Hwy 24**. Go approximately 3 miles on **Hwy 24 west**, then turn **left into France Park**. Follow the **Park Entrance Road** 0.5 miles to the **parking area** at the **"Frisbee Golf"** sign on the **right**.

Farther along, the trail crosses the handicap-accessible path that leads to the back half of the fishing quarry. The path begins from reserved handicap spaces off the main road and ends at a ramped viewing area for individuals to view the wild birds roosting in trees sprouting from the quarry. From this perch, great blue herons can be seen patiently waiting to catch their day's meal. (More information on the area's plants and wildlife can be found at the wildlife observation building.)

The trails of France Park provide cyclists with a variety of terrain and trail surfaces. Rolling across the dry quarry is like riding on a rough gravel road. Once the trail climbs out of the quarry, a smooth pea gravel path eases toward the swimming area and acts as a nice transition to the singletrack.

Hang on!

As the singletrack edges the swimming quarry, the trail hosts several challenging climbs and one particularly challenging descent. After the descent the trail begins to resemble a mountain biker's version of the spring road racing classic, Paris Roubaix— *The Hell of the North*. Cobblestones are replaced with limestone nubs, making an interesting view as well as a challenge to negotiate.

Once through this technical section, the trail mellows, descends to the perimeter of a field, then eases down to the Wabash River. A non-threatening uphill along a gravel road leads away from the river and back to the singletrack.

The trail crosses a wooden bridge and changes surface again. Resembling a hamster cage, wood chips spring under the rolling tires. This doubletrack trail leads to the last challenging section of singletrack that edges the perimeter of the fishing pond. The singletrack merges with a paved trail and meanders past the falls then back to the parking area.

Several trails northwest of the swimming pond are favorites for beginning riders, where a trace of the old Erie Canal can be ridden. Riders should take caution, though—avoid this area during wet weather. This swampy section is rarely dry, and those nasty nettles grow strong and thick.

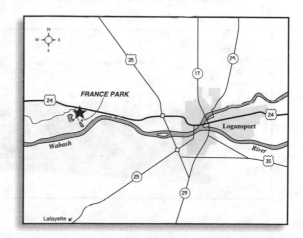

MILES   DIRECTIONS

0.0   **START** at the **parking area** above the **waterfalls**. Turn **right** out of parking area and follow the main park road.

0.05   Turn **left** before the park road splits, and cross to the trailhead. The trail descends to the bottom of the dry quarry.

0.1   Pass a trail that goes off to the right. Continue **straight,** following the perimeter of the dry quarry.

0.3   Pass an ascent out of the quarry. Continue **straight** on the **PERIMETER TRAIL**. Ride across a limestone tabletop trail, then climb up a rock-studded ascent.

0.4   Turn **right** onto a **PEA GRAVEL PATH**. Follow the well-groomed trail through the campsites and down to the **Swimming Quarry beach**.

0.6   Trail merges with a gravel road. Follow the **GRAVEL ROAD** down to the beach area.

0.8   Follow the road through the **gravel beach parking** lot.

0.88   Take the road to the left out of the parking lot.

0.9   Shift into your granny gear and take a quick **right** onto singletrack.

0.95   Stay on the trail that veers to the right as it passes a faint trail to the left.

1.1   Pass a trail to the right that descends to the beach.

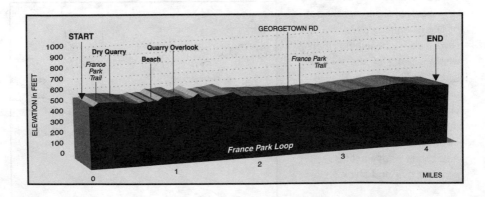

Most Difficult
Difficult
Moderate
Easy

START

FRANCE   PARK

Observation
Area

Water Falls

Dry
Quarry

Canal

Fishing

Quarry

Erie

Beach

Swimming

Quarry

Outhouses

Field

Field

Field

Pines

New Trees

0

½ MILE

River

ROAD

GEORGETOWN

Wabash

SOUTH   RIVER   ROAD   WEST

1.18   Pass a trail that leads to the quarry's edge.

1.2   Turn **right** off the **MAIN TRAIL** to the ledge overlooking the **Swimming Quarry**.

1.3   This scenic trail merges back to the **MAIN TRAIL**. There is a tricky descent just after the trails merge.

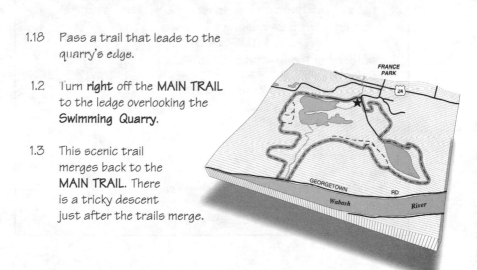

Limestone lining this singletrack is similar to the cobblestones of old European farm roads.

1.5   The trail splits near the edge of the quarry. Follow the **MAIN TRAIL** to the **left**.

1.55   The trail bends to the right then arrives at a "T." Turn **left**.

1.6   Arrive at a trail intersection. Turn **left**. Turning right leads back to the swimming area.

1.9   Arrive at a trail intersection. Turn **left** on a doubletrack path. This trail descends.

2.0   Turn right at the bottom of the descent before the trail goes into an open field. Immediately arrive at a trail intersection. Continue **straight** taking the trail with the **large rock** at the trailhead.

2.1   Pass the **red outhouse**. The trail now travels along flat, easy terrain.

2.2   Arrive at a trail intersection. Continue **straight**.

2.4   Arrive at a trail split marked by the **green outhouse**. Take the **left** split.

2.5   Turn **right** on **GEORGETOWN ROAD**.

Ride Information

Trail Maintenance Hotline:
Cass County Parks & Recreation   (219) 753-2928
    4505 W. US 24 West
    Logansport, IN 46947-9083

Scuba Diving in the Quarry:
Diving Den, Inc.   (317) 452-1034
    2229 E. County Road 00 North
    East Markland Ave.
    Kokomo, IN 46901

Park Schedule:
Open dawn to dusk, year-round

Cost:
$4.00 per person; $100 for a season pass

Maps:
USGS maps: Clymers, IN; Lucerne, IN

2.55 Turn **right** onto the **gravel driveway** across from the **France Park Access Site** for the Wabash River. Climb the **GRAVEL ACCESS ROAD**.

Nettle Tea

1. Mix two cups of water with a handful of nettle leaves. The amount of leaves will vary the strength of the tea.
2. Bring the water to a boil.
3. Let simmer for ten minutes.
4. Strain the leaves when pouring. Enjoy.

2.6 Turn **left** at the top of the climb. The singletrack cuts through the woods.

2.8 Pass a trail that takes a 120-degree turn to the right, and take the **next right**. This is a nice run through pine trees with a pine-needle carpet. The trail crosses a small field.

3.0 Arrive at a trail intersection. Continue **straight**.

3.1 The trail arrives at a "T." Turn **left**.

3.45 Cross a **wooden bridge** over the old **Erie Canal** and pass a singletrack trail to the right. Now on the woodchip portion of the trail.

3.5 The trail arrives at a "T." Turn **left**.

3.8 Arrive at a **trail intersection**. Go **straight** at the trail intersection onto technical singletrack. Now following the **north rim** of the **fishing quarry**.

4.0 Cross the paved path to the **observation area**. Continue **straight** on singletrack.

4.1 The **MAIN TRAIL** merges with the paved path. Take a **right** on the path and follow it back to the falls and parking area.

4.2 Arrive back at the waterfalls.

6   Wildcat Valley Park

Ride Specs

Start: Trailhead near caretaker's home

Length: 1.9 miles

Rating: Moderate

Terrain: Grassy, wooded singletrack

Riding Time: 20+ minutes

Other Uses: Camping, tennis, putt-putt golf, basketball

Named after Miami Chief Kokomoko, the city of Kokomo is better known as the "City of Firsts." The pneumatic rubber tire, the carburetor, the American Howitzer, the all-transistor car radio, and the first commercially built gasoline-powered car in Indiana all were born in this city.

One man in particular was a driving force in this invention-crazed city. In 1894, Elwood Haynes drove into history when he took his first test drive around the streets of Kokomo. Actually, his car was towed three miles outside the city so not to disturb the horse-drawn carriages within the city limits. The first drive was successful and Haynes went on to invent a number of other items.

His primary interest, though, was metallurgy. Haynes has a claim to the invention of stainless steel, as well as the invention of stellite—a high performance nickel chromium alloy. The development of this alloy led to the construction of the Stellite Corporation.

Haynes has a museum named after him, his house is a historical monument, and Wildcat Park was once his own. The recreational area was built in 1957 and used by the employees of Haynes International—what used to be the Stellite plant.

They built a softball diamond, shuffleboard courts, horseshoe pits, a putt-putt

Don't fall to your right!

Getting There

☞ **From downtown Kokomo** – Take **Sycamore Road/Hwy 22** west 9 miles to **County Road 900 West**. Turn **left** on **County Road 900 West** and travel one mile to **County Road OO North/South**. Turn **right** on **County Road OO North/South** and travel 0.5 miles to **County Road 950 West**. Turn **left** on **County Road 950 West** and travel 0.5 miles to the **Wildcat Valley Park Entrance**. Turn **right** into the park and follow the **Park Entrance Road** to the **parking area**.

---

golf course, and the buildings on the site, all of which are still here today.

As younger employees moved up through the company, the park received less support and was abandoned. In the early 1980s, a group of firemen and policemen initiated a corporation to buy and refurbish the park, which was to be dubbed the Law Enforcement/Firefighters Recreational Park. But since the majority of investors were civilians, the investors voted for the name Wildcat Park.

A local mountain bike enthusiast approached the caretakers about constructing trails in the park. Working together, they cut a loop that follows the perimeter of the property.

Starting near the caretaker's house, the trail hides just behind the treeline and leads to the front gate. Winding down the edge of the trees and the tennis court, the trail remains flat and acts as a nice warm-up for the singletrack.

Approaching the creek, the trail dips quickly and becomes more challenging. Using the most of a limited landscape, the trail has multiple creek crossings in addition to many climbs and descents on the hill that edges Wildcat Creek. On the ridgetop, and just behind the main lodge, the trail edges a swampy area. The caretakers first believed this was an environmental problem surfacing on their property. As it turns out, it was a natural spring. One of the original landowners told the caretakers how she used to plow the fields with a horse-drawn plow. She also revealed to them this spring in which she used to water her horses.

Past the spring, the trail then dives back to the creek's bank and follows the low path. A short climb leads to the trailhead, which completes the loop in just under two miles.

The caretakers hope to add more trails in the future. In the meantime, local cyclists have been given a

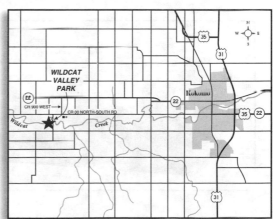

moderate course to enjoy where they can prepare for the two mountain bike races that stop here each year.

After the ride, take Highway 22 back into town and make a stop at the Victory Bike Shop—a museum of sorts. The shop opened in 1936 and Charles Sullivan started working there three years later. Charles now acts as the shop's curator, owner, and expert mechanic. Lining the walls of the shop are bicycles of a bygone era. Some of the exhibits include a 1937 Monarch Silver King Deluxe, a 1939 Schwinn used to set the former land speed record, a chromeless Victory bike, a boneshaker, and a 7½-foot-tall lamplighter's bicycle. The only other antique, boasts the owner, is Charles himself.

Other sites to see before leaving Kokomo include Old Ben and the Sycamore Stump. It seems Old Ben was a crossbred Hereford that weighed 4,270 pounds and stood six feet, four inches tall. The town so loved Ben that they had him stuffed. Paul Bunyan's Babe has nothing on Ben. The Sycamore Stump is what remains of a great Sycamore tree with a circumference of 51 feet. The tree was damaged during a storm in 1915. The stump was later hollowed out, placed in a park, and used as a telephone booth.

If the phone were still there, you could use it to call home, because with all of this riding and sightseeing, you will surely be running late!

MILES   DIRECTIONS

0.0   **START** at the **trailhead** near the **caretaker's home**. Leave the parking area and ride across the grassy field next to the **caretaker's house**.

0.05   Find the trailhead at the treeline. Immediately arrive at a **trail intersection**. Take the trail to the **right**.

0.2   The trail bends to the **right**, paralleling **County Road 950 West**. Roll **straight** across a grassy field and cross the paved entrance to the camp.

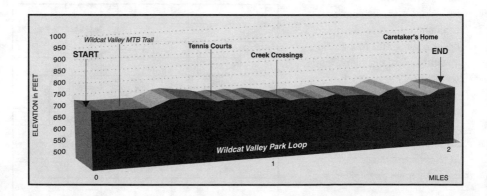

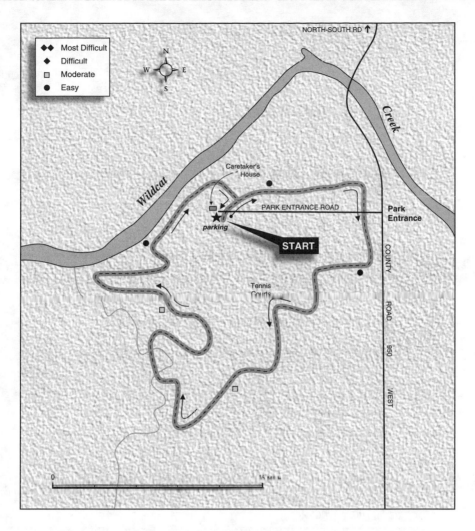

0.3 Continue across the grassy field and find the trailhead at the treeline.

0.4 The trail bends to the right.

0.5 The trail heads off to the left just before emptying out into a grassy field.

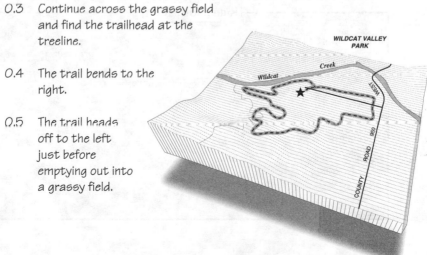

0.55   The trail bends to the right and straddles the treeline and a cornfield.

0.6   The trail rolls behind the **tennis courts**.

0.7   The actual trail is faint here. Turn **left** at the **storage building** and follow the edge of the grassy area. The trailhead is straight ahead.

0.75   The trail heads off to the right. The trailhead is marked by an old **Coke machine** on the left.

0.8   The trail splits. Take the **left split**.

0.9   Leave the wide grassy trail and turn **right** onto **singletrack**.

1.0   The trail crosses a **creek**.

1.2   The trail crosses the **creek** a second time.

1.3   The trail splits. Take the **left split**.

1.4   The singletrack dumps out into an open area. Turn **left** along the treeline to find the trailhead.

1.5   The trail heads off to the right. Continue **straight** on the **main trail**. The trail that heads off to the right leads to the bathhouse.

1.6   The trail splits. Take the **left split** and begin a climb. The trail tops out with the parking lot in sight. Turn **left** and follow the treeline to the trailhead.

Ride Information

Trail Maintenance Hotline:
    Caretakers   (317) 883-5207
Park Schedule:
    Open daily, from sunrise to sunset
Cost:
    $3 per person
Victory Bike Shop: (317) 452-9717
    107 E. Sycamore St
    Kokomo, IN 46901
Maps:
    USGS map: Russiaville, IN

Look at that chainring! This land-speed-record-setting Schwinn was used back in 1939. Check it out at the Victory Bike Shop "museum" in Kokomo.

1.7 The trail empties out into an open area with the parking lot in sight. Follow the treeline to the left toward the trailhead.

1.8 The trail bends to the right, climbs, and tops out at the beginning of loop. Cyclists have the option of riding back to parking area or taking another loop around the Wildcat Valley Park trail.

1.9 Reach the end of the ride.

7 Prairie Creek Reservoir

Ride Specs

Start: Trail parking area

Length: 7-mile trail system

Rating: Moderate

Terrain: Rocky, scrub singletrack and doubletrack

Riding Time: 30 minutes – 1½ hours

Other Uses: Camping, ATV, fishing, windsurfing, swimming

Named after the "Munsee" clan of the Delaware Indians, Muncie became a hotbed of activity when natural gas was discovered for the second time just north of town. When natural gas was tapped for the first time by oil drillers in 1876, it had little economic value because few people knew its potential, and the site was closed. Ten years later, the Eaton Well was reopened when natural gas was deemed a worthy fossil fuel. By 1890, 226 industries had flocked to Delaware County and the city of Muncie.

Adopting the moniker "Gas City of the West," Muncie attracted glass-jar manufacturer Frank Ball to move his business from Buffalo, New York, after a fire destroyed his family's factory. More than 100 years later, the Ball Corporation is the oldest, continuously operating home canning jar manufacturer in the world.

In 1918, this philanthropic family went on to purchase the 64 acres and two buildings of the failing Muncie Normal Institute and presented it as a gift to the state. Four years later, the state thanked the family by naming the

Getting There

☞ **From downtown Muncie** – Go **east** on **West Jackson Road**, traveling 0.8 miles to **Ohio Street** and turn **right**. At the next intersection, **Ohio Street** becomes **Burlington Street**. Continue **straight** on **Burlington Street**. Drive 3.6 miles and turn **left** on **Inlow Springs Road**, following signs for **Camp Munsee** and **Prairie Creek Reservoir**. Inlow Springs Road becomes **Windsor Road** after the crossing the **White River**. Drive 2.1 miles and turn **right** on **County Road 475 East**. Follow **County Road 475 East** 2.1 miles, then turn **left** on **County Road 500 South**. Drive 0.1 miles and turn **right** on **County Road 462 East**. Travel 1.4 miles on **County Road 462 East** and turn **left** on **County Road 50 South**. Drive 0.1 miles and turn **left** into the **Prairie Creek Trailhead Parking Area**. Follow the dirt road to the widened parking area.

school in their honor, calling it Ball State Teachers College. By 1965, the college had widened its class offering, gained university status, and is now known as Ball State University.

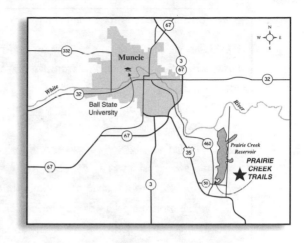

The Statue of Benefi-cence stands on campus as a tribute to the Ball's generosity. Known as "Benny," the winged angel holds a gift of jewels with five columns standing behind her. Each column represents one of the five Ball brothers.

Ball State is also known for one of its most famous alumni, David Letterman. In the spirit of our favorite hometown comedian, alumni, and local boy turned good, please see the Top Ten list for mountain biking the Prairie Creek trail system (see sidebar on page 76).

As you enter the trail area, there is a sign that lists the charges for trail use. This sign is for motorcycles only. Mountain biking is free!

Prairie Creek's trails represent another example of a spider-webbed maze of singletrack and off-road wonder. Make your own loop or attempt to follow the elusive DINO route. The Do INdiana Off-road race series makes two stops here during their season and somehow manages to squeeze a racing loop from this labyrinth of trails.

The trails cover ground where there once was a gravel pit. The terrain is rough, stony, and full of scrub brush. Small growth trees, briars, and other low-lying shrubs seem to be the only vegetation capable of growing here.

A two-mile perimeter loop can be run by always choosing the farthermost left trail when traveling clockwise. This loop winds around the perimeter of this network of trails and follows the edges of the 1,250-acre reservoir. This loop is preferred when there are lots of motorcycles using the trails.

The shores of Prairie Creek Reservoir.

Top Ten Reasons for Riding the Prairie Creek Trail System

10. Optional motorpacing sessions offered by local ATV trail riders.

9. Can earn nursing credits from Ball State for dressing a gravel wound.

8. Professors encourage students to ditch class and go mountain biking at Prairie Creek.

7. Can earn cartography credits from Ball State for attempting to map every trail at Prairie Creek.

6. Delapidated root cellar at the northeast section of the trail system doubles as a walk-in beer cooler.

5. Munsee Clan based tribal hierarchy on annual Prairie Creek mountain bike race.

4. Great testing grounds for off-road equipment bought with textbook money.

3. Charlie Cardinal unwinds here after big games.

2. Dodging pesky motorcycles increases agility.

1. Frank Ball rode to Prairie Creek's highest point and proclaimed, "This is where I will rebuild my family's business!"

Motorcycle riders seem to stay on the wider trails and avoid this tight section. If they do venture back on this loop, they seem to ride it at a reduced speed, which makes being passed a less frightening experience.

One interesting site, found at the northeast end of the trail system overlooking the reservoir, is the remains of what appears to be a root cellar. It is little more than a hole cut in the side of the hill supported by a stone entrance. The structure stirs the imagination to wonder what stood on this point in years past.

Prairie Creek is a convenient and somewhat challenging loop for Ball State

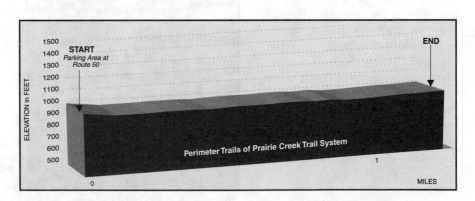

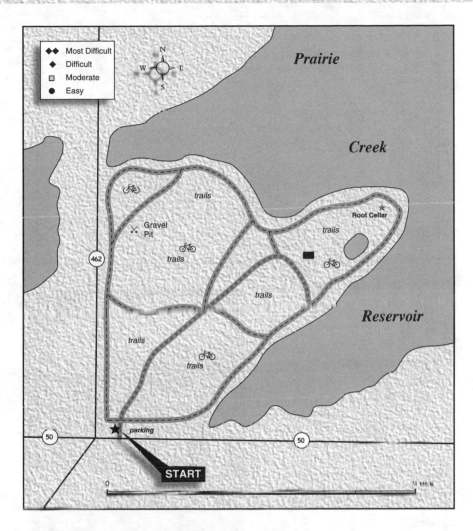

- ◆◆ Most Difficult
- ◆ Difficult
- ☐ Moderate
- ● Easy

N W E S

Prairie

Creek

trails

Gravel Pit

Root Cellar

trails

462

trails

trails

Reservoir

trails

trails

trails

50

50

parking

START

0   ¼ mile

students and Muncie residents. It is also a prime example of how quickly an unmanaged trail system can be destroyed. Mountain bikers can thank ATV and motorcycle riders for creating the trails, but these motorized vehicles could also slowly be destroying their own creation!

This is a sensitive area and can really accommodate only a few trails crisscrossing through it. The problem, though, is honeycombing and continuously widening trails that result whenever puddles form in the middle of

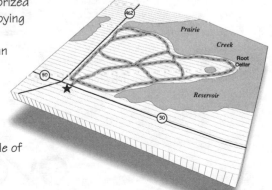

Ride Information

Trail Maintenance Hotline:
Muncie Park and Recreation Office   (317) 747-4776
Prairie Creek Parks Department
c/o City Hall
300 N. High Street
Muncie, IN 47305
Ball State University   (317) 289-1241
2000 W. University Ave.
Muncie, IN 47306-1022
Schedule:
Prairie Creek Trails open from dawn till dusk, year-round
Maps:
USGS map: Mount Pleasant, IN

the trail. The trails are so tight that a trail intersection is crossed every 20 feet. There is some singletrack here, but trails that could allow a truck to pass through seem to be the most predominant.

Already erosion is in high gear and is particularly noticeable on the climbs at the northeast corner of the trail system. Two-foot trenches have been carved into the top of each of the four climbs now cutting into the hill.

With the state's limited trail systems, especially in the northern portion of the state, a trail adoption program would serve as an option to keep this system open and rideable. Cyclists could work with ATV and motorcycle riders to preserve Prairie Creek before it becomes another trail-closure statistic.

Statue of Beneficence, or "Benny," on campus at Ball State University.

96th Street Station Trail 8

John Matthews, owner of Bicycle Outfitters, had some insight when he opened his bike shop at 96th Street Station Shopping Center. From the back door of his store, customers can ride the best legal trail system in the city of Indianapolis. If cyclists are interested in an introduction to the 96th Street Station loop or simply looking to ride with other cyclists, group rides leave the shop every Sunday at 5:30 p.m., daylight providing. Extending his version of Hoosier hospitality, John even leaves a hose outside the back door for cyclists to wash off their bikes after a hard ride.

The trail crosses four different owners' property: The state of Indiana, the city of Fishers, a private pipeline company, and a private individual, each of whom own a portion of the trail. Thankfully, no complications have arisen to keep mountain bikers from enjoying these scenic trails.

Ride Specs

Start: Bicycle Outfitters

Length: 3.8 miles of 6-mile system

Rating: Easy to Moderate

Terrain: Woods, fields, singletrack, dirt roads

Riding Time: 1 – 2 hours

Other Uses: Hiking, fishing

Group rides leave from here every Sunday at 5:30 p.m.

Getting There

☞ **From the northeast side of Indianapolis** – Take **Allisonville Road north** from I-465 1.1 miles to the **96ᵗʰ Street Station Shopping Center**. Turn **left** into the **parking lot** and drive around to the back of **Bicycle Outfitters**. Park here.

Some local cyclists marked the trails with signs in hopes of improving the safety of the tight singletrack sections. Bridges over swampy areas were constructed and "One Way" directional signs were placed at critical points along the loop.

To ensure the safety of other cyclists, please follow the "One Way" signs on the singletrack sections of this trail. Because this ride is so close to a metropolitan area, it has become a high-traffic route. The unidirectional singletrack allows cyclists to focus on improving bike-handling skills without worrying about getting involved in high-speed mountain bike collisions.

The 96ᵗʰ Street Station Trail begins by dropping off the back of Bicycle Outfitters' parking lot. The singletrack descent bottoms out at a creekbed, crosses Old 96ᵗʰ Street, then climbs up a small ridgetop. The path rolls and winds for nearly one mile before dumping into a flat field cut with dirt roads.

This portion of the ride offers a short break before diving back into the woods. The following section is a relatively flat, winding singletrack that leads to the pipeline trail. This straight section contains a mild descent, bringing cyclists to the edge of the White River. From here on out, the trail remains a short distance from the river as it heads toward Old 96ᵗʰ Street. The trail heads back to the bike shop, but not without one last hill that tops out at Bicycle Outfitters' back door.

Along the 96ᵗʰ Street Station loop, two sites provide an alternative to cycling. One-half of a mile into the ride, the singletrack threads across a

hilltop around a Civil War-era cemetery. The oldest, legible gravestone dates back to 1870. With the gravesite set up seemingly in the middle of nowhere, you may wonder who buried their relatives here, and where those descendants are now.

The second stop is found along the banks of the White River. Two and one-half miles into the ride, a great rope swing dangles from a hefty tree branch. With the proper windup, you could splash down 20 feet from the bank.

After the ride, cyclists may be faced with a difficult decision — deciding whether to enjoy a cold brew at

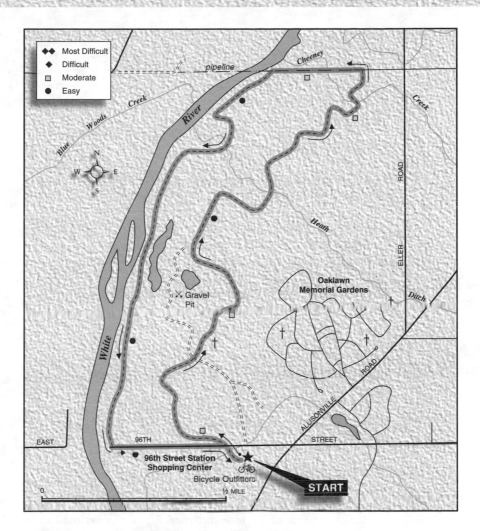

the 96th Street Pub or grab a chicken salad bagel sandwich at D'Amicos Bagels. Choosing between the two can be as difficult as racing for the lead on narrow singletrack.

Post-ride disputes aside, this trail system provides Indianapolis cyclists a challenging ride without a lengthy commute. During the week, area cyclists can easily drive to the trailhead, ride a couple of loops, grab a beer or bagel, and be home by eight o'clock.

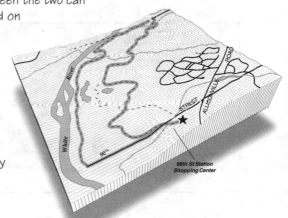

MILES   DIRECTIONS

0.0   **START** at the **Bicycle Outfitters Bike Shop**. Find the trailhead behind Bicycle Outfitters at the edge of the parking lot. The trail dives downhill toward a small creek.

0.15 The trail crosses a creek and later, a utility path. Continue **straight** on singletrack.

0.1   The trail intersects with a **dirt road (Old 96TH Street)**. Turn **left** on OLD 96TH STREET.

0.11 Look for the trailhead marker on the right of the road that reads: *Attention mountain bikers: Please follow directional signs. Indicate safer riding. Thank you.* Turn **right** onto the SINGLETRACK TRAIL.

0.15 The trail splits. Take the **right split**.

0.3   The trail dumps out into an open field, then does a hairpin before returning to the woods.

0.4   The trail crosses a **small dirt road**. Continue **straight** on SINGLETRACK.

0.5   The trail passes an **old cemetery**. The oldest grave that is legible, dates back to 1870.

0.7   The trail passes a **ten-foot fence** topped with barbed wire. Follow the trail around the fence.

0.8   The trail intersects with a **wide dirt road**. Follow the **dirt road** to the **right**.

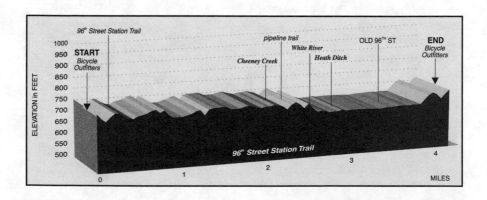

0.95   Come to a **dirt road intersection**. Turn **right** on the DIRT ROAD. Now heading toward a sewage treatment plant.

1.05   Find the trailhead on the left. Follow the **SINGLETRACK PATH** to the **left**.

1.2   Cross **Heath Ditch**.

1.9   A trail merges in from the left. Stay on the **main trail** and **veer to the right**.

2.1   The trail crosses a dirt road on a diagonal. Continue **straight** on singletrack.

2.2   The trail crosses a **dirt road**. Continue **straight** on singletrack.

2.25   The trail crosses **Cheeney Creek**.

2.3   Arrive at a **trail intersection**. Turn **left**. Now on the **PIPELINE** portion of the trail.

2.5   Turn **left** off the pipeline section. The White River is now in view.

2.6   The trail bends to the **left**. Now following the river bank.

2.65   Cross an open area along the river bank. Cyclists can take a break here to swing on the rope swing and plunge into the river. On quiet days, this is also a great spot to see great blue herons wading upstream.

2.7 Come to a singletrack trail on the right. Leave doubletrack and take the **SINGLETRACK TRAIL** to the **right**.

2.75 The singletrack path intersects with a **dirt road**. Turn **right** on the **DIRT ROAD**.

2.8 Cross **Heath Ditch**. Take an immediate **right** on the path marked with a **red One Way arrow**.

2.85 The singletrack path dumps out onto a dirt road. Turn **left** on the **DIRT ROAD**. Follow the river's edge.

2.9 Take the **SINGLETRACK TRAIL** to the **right** at the trailhead marked with a **red "One Way" arrow**.

2.95 The trail crosses a **dirt road**. Continue **straight** on the singletrack.

3.1 Arrive at a trail split. Take the **left split**.

3.2 Arrive at a **trail intersection**. Continue **straight** on the singletrack.

3.4 The trail changes to doubletrack. Continue **straight** on the **DOUBLETRACK TRAIL**, continuing to follow the river.

3.41 The trail splits. Take the **right split**.

3.45 Come to a faint trail split. Take the **right split**, continuing to follow the riverbank.

Ride Information

Trail Maintenance Hotline:
Bicycle Outfitters   (317) 842-BIKE (2453)
    9546 Allisonville Road, Suite 113
Indianapolis, IN 46250

Group Ride Schedule:
Group rides leave from Bicycle Outfitters every Sunday at 5:30 p.m., daylight providing

Maps:
USGS map: Fishers, IN

3.5   Arrive at an intersection with a dirt road **(Old 96TH Street)**. Turn **left** on OLD 96TH STREET.

3.6   Arrive at a **trail intersection.** Continue **straight** on the OLD 96TH STREET.

3.7   Arrive at a **trail intersection.** Turn **right** off OLD 96TH STREET onto **singletrack.** Shift into your granny gear and climb back to the parking lot behind Bicycle Outfitters.

3.8   Ride complete. Now let's go shopping at the bike store!

9 River's Edge Trail

Ride Specs

Start: Bicycle Garage of Indianapolis

Length: 4.2 miles

Rating: Easy

Terrain: Flat; singletrack

Riding Time: 30 minutes – 1 hour

Other Uses: Hiking, jogging, fitness stations

Indianapolis is in a dilemma when it comes to mountain biking. It holds the highest number of mountain bikers in the state, yet holds the least number of legal trail systems. Granted, Indianapolis is topographically-challenged, but there are a few geological wrinkles on the northeast side of town that provide good terrain for mountain bikes. The challenge, however, is in getting the approval needed to open some of these public and private lands to mountain biking. And this burden can be attributed, in part, to cyclists themselves.

The trails of Fort Benjamin Harrison are a prime example of a trail system recently closed down because of cyclists' disregard for the property on which they rode. Officials have documented separate incidents in which cyclists washed their muddy bikes in the fort's showers and taunted troops during military maneuvers. With these black marks against mountain bikers, the upper brass will not be opening this system anytime soon.

With the emergence of responsible riders, though, there is a chance these trails will be reopened in the future. One reason for this growth of responsibility is the Indiana mountain biker's recently acquired political power with representation in the Indiana Bicycle Coalition. Political force coupled with the fashionable insurgence of low-impact riding hopefully will lead to more land being opened to off-road cycling in the future.

In the meantime, local cyclists must be content to ride such places as

Getting There

☞   **From downtown Indianapolis** – Take **Meridian Street north** approximately 11 miles to **I-465**. Take **I-465 east** 2 miles to **Keystone Avenue (Exit 33)**. Go **south** on **Keystone Avenue** 0.6 miles to **82nd Street**. Travel **east** on **82nd Street** approximately 1 mile to the **River's Edge Shopping Center**. Turn **left** into the **parking lot** and park at the east end of the shopping center next to the **Bicycle Garage of Indianapolis**.

the River's Edge trails. Located behind the River's Edge Shopping Center, these trails serve more as a mountain bike test-ride trail for customers and employees at the Bicycle Garage than a long ride in the national forest. In fact, the owners of the Bicycle Garage helped design this trail system and host rides here every Wednesday at 5:30 p.m. Please call in advance for more details.

There are a few miles of singletrack that wind behind the store and lead up to Riverbend Apartments, located on the north side of I-465. It appears that these trails might connect with the 96th Street Station trails someday, but as of yet, River's Edge still remains an out-and-back loop.

For beginners, this is a non-threatening loop where cyclists can get their feet wet with some basic singletrack. There are no substantial climbs, but very few straight sections. Thus, bike handling skills can be improved as cyclists pedal through this short course. There is also a jogging path edging Lake Allisonville that has been incorporated into the trail and offers a break from the singletrack.

For cyclists working on the northeast side of town, this trail

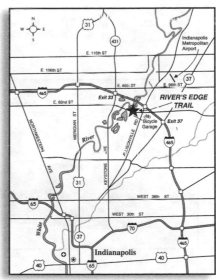

system serves as a perfect lunchtime or evening workout loop. Carve the trails for 45 minutes, then grab some food from one of the many area eateries.

On the north side of I-465, cyclists will come across a number of fitness stations. Fitness fanatics can dismount their bicycles and perform the recommended fitness activities if the trails don't provide enough stimulation.

For a more difficult ride, some challenging obstacles are found on the trail directly behind the Bicycle Garage. There are two ditches that offer short steep drops which bottom out and are immediately followed with a short climb. Test your skills while attempting to ride over a downed tree, and finish this technical section with a short climb up to the parking lot. This section can either be avoided or sought out, depending on the level of difficulty for which you are looking.

Overall, the trail is tight, winding, and surrounded by tall weeds on much of the trail. There is two-way traffic throughout, and accidents can be avoided by keeping your speed in check.

MILES DIRECTIONS

0.0 **START** at the **Bicycle Garage of Indianapolis**. There are two trailheads. One is directly behind the Bicycle Garage and the other is located at the far east end of the parking lot. Take the **trailhead** at the **far east end**.

0.31 The trail splits. Take the **right split**.

0.45 Pass a trail on the right. Stay on the **MAIN TRAIL** to the left.

0.5 Arrive at a **multi-trail intersection**. Take the **MAIN TRAIL straight** through this intersection.

0.55 The **MAIN TRAIL** bears to the **right**.

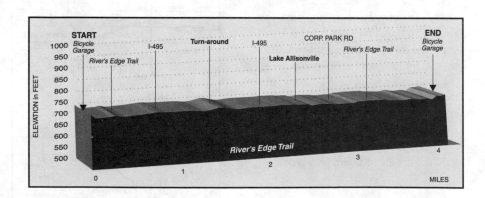

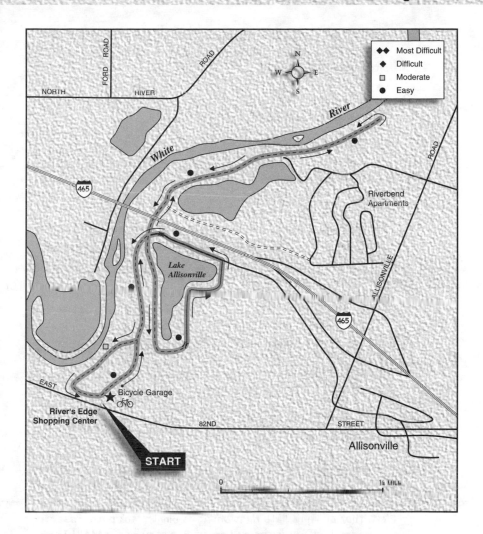

0.6   The **MAIN TRAIL** intersects with a larger trail. Turn **left. Lake Allisonville** and I-**465** now in view. Pass a **bridge** on the right and continue **straight** on the MAIN TRAIL.

0.7   Pass under I-**465**. Continue **straight** on the trail.

0.75   The trail splits. Take the **MAIN TRAIL** to the **right**.

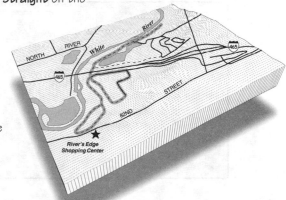

0.8   A small trail splits off to the right. Stay on the MAIN TRAIL to the left. Pass many small trails on the left and right. But continue on the MAIN TRAIL.

1.2   The trail splits. Take the **left split**. The right split leads to the tennis courts of Riverbend Apartments.

1.3   The trail splits. Take the right split. Travel 0.3 miles and take a 180-degree turn. The trail passes many small trails and splits, but the main trail is easy to identify. Take the main trail back under I-465.

2.0   The trail splits just as it passes the **wooden bridge**. Take the **left split** around the lake. The right trail leads back to the Bicycle Garage.

2.4   The trail splits. Take the **left split** following the perimeter of **Lake Allisonville**.

2.5   Cross a **wooden bridge**. The trail becomes a **paved path**.

2.8   The trail intersects with a corporate park road. Turn **left** on the CORPORATE PARK ROAD.

2.82   Look for the "Fitness Trail" sign on the right. Turn **right** onto the FITNESS TRAIL.

3.0   The jogging path splits. Take the **left split**. Now paralleling I-465.

3.5   Cross a **wooden bridge** and arrive at a **trail intersection**. Turn **left**, then an immediate **right** onto the **singletrack path**. Pass many small intersections and splits, but stay on the MAIN TRAIL.

Ride Information

Trail Maintenance Hotline:
   Bicycle Garage of Indianapolis   (317) 842-4140
      4130 East 82nd Street
      Indianapolis, IN 46250
Group Ride Schedule:
   Group rides leave from Bicycle Garage every Wednesday at 5:30 p.m., daylight providing
Maps:
   USGS map: Fishers, IN

3.9   The trail splits. Take the **right split.** Now approaching the challeng-
       ing section of the loop.

4.1   Cross a ditch and arrive at a **trail intersection**. Take the MAIN
       TRAIL to the **right**.

4.15   The trail splits. Take the **right split** and climb a hill to return to
       the parking lot of the **Bicycle Garage**.

4.2   Ride complete.

10 Indianapolis Water Co. Canal

Ride Specs

Start: Heslar Naval Armory

Length: 5 miles

Rating: Easy

Terrain: Flat; canal towpath

Riding Time: 1½ – 2 hours

Other Uses: Walking, running, fishing, feeding ducks

Transportation in Indiana's early days was difficult at best. Not yet established as the crossroads of America, Indiana had only the National Road (today's Highway 40) crossing through to connect it with the rest of the Union.

During this era of river transportation, dignified riverboat pilots like Mark Twain steered majestic steamboats through the state's major rivers. Riverboats paddling along the Ohio and Wabash Rivers brought commerce to sleepy river towns and turned them into glitzy social centers.

Therefore, local legislators believed that digging canals would capitalize on this transportation trend and connect Indiana with these river towns and the rest of the country.

In fact, the Central Canal, constructed in Indianapolis, was originally designed to be a connector route to the Wabash and Erie Canals. The goal was to link Indiana with New York City and New Orleans. If connected to these major commerce centers, Hoosiers could trade goods and cutting edge ideas, and, more importantly, become a contributing factor in the country's industrial rise.

Unfortunately, only nine miles were completed before the project was abandoned. The completion of the canal depended on revenues generated from canal commerce. The lack of revenue, political fraud and embezzlement, and the emergence of railroads killed the fanfare surrounding this grand project.

Other than a grand ceremonial voyage back in 1837, the Central Canal has seen little boat traffic. It has seen its share of recreational traffic, though. Years ago, members of the now defunct Wheelway League pedaled along the

Getting There

☞ **From downtown Indianapolis** – Take **I-65 north** to **29th/30th Street (Exit 116)**. Take **West 30th Street** approximately 1.5 miles to **White River Drive East**. Go **north** on **White River Drive East** and park along the side of the road near **Heslar Naval Armory**.

Cycling along the Indy Water Company Canal towpath.

towpath while young lovers paddled their canoes through the slow-moving water.

Today, the Central Canal is called the Indianapolis Water Company Canal. As the canal's ownership has changed, so has the challenges of today's cyclists. One such challenge is finding a parking space. The best chances for parking are at the Heslar Naval Armory at the southern end of the maintained canal trail. There is less traffic and plenty of free parking, and no time is lost searching for limited, costly parking at the other end of the path in Broad Ripple.

Once on the trail, cyclists will pass many notable sites, including the canal itself. How ironic it is that this botched canal project is one of the longest stretches of canal left in the state. Even the mighty Erie Canal, which we sung about as children, has been reduced to mere traces and empty indentions.

Near the trailhead, Marian College and the Major Taylor Velodrome are just a stone's throw away. Marian is note-worthy for cyclists in that it is one of only two colleges in the country to offer bicycle racing scholarships.

A distinct advantage for the Marian team is having the Major Taylor Velodrome right across the street. This homecourt advantage has raised Marian to one of the country's top bike racing schools, including having the distinction of being the 1995 National Track Champions.

As the trail crosses under 38th Street, cyclists have a decision to make: continue along the trail, visit the Indianapolis Museum of Art, or visit James Whitcomb Riley's gravesite at Crown Hill Cemetery. While the museum is just on the other side of the canal, Crown Hill Cemetery is a little farther east on 38th Street, past Michigan Avenue. If you have the time, take in a little culture, or bask in the spectacular view of the city from Riley's hilltop gravesite at the county's highest point. Tradition also warrants that you leave a few pennies on the grave (see sidebar on page 97).

MILES   DIRECTIONS

0.0   START at the Heslar Naval Armory. Leave your parking space and ride to the intersection of White River Drive East and West 30th Street. Turn left and travel east on WEST 30th STREET.

0.2   Turn left before crossing the canal onto the CANAL TOWPATH, marked by a blue gate.

0.75   Pass under I-65.

1.2   Pass under East 38th Street.

1.3   Pass the Indiana Art Museum on the opposite side of the canal. During the summer you may often find jazz concerts on the back steps of the museum.

1.4   Pass a trail on the left. There is a loop back there, but mountain biking is prohibited.

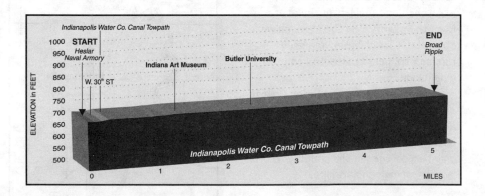

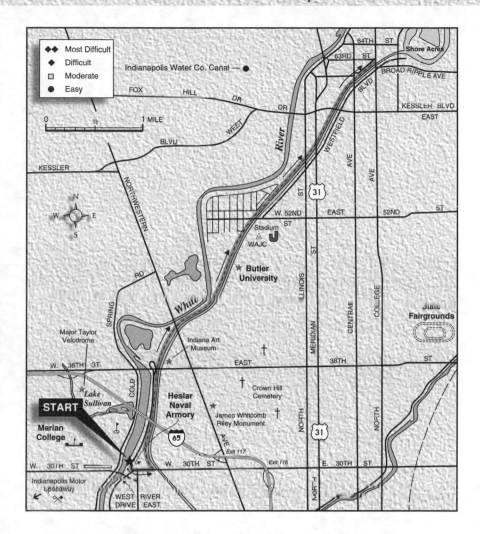

Legend:
- ◆◆ Most Difficult
- ◆ Difficult
- □ Moderate
- ● Easy

Indianapolis Water Co. Canal — ●

0   ½   1 MILE

1.6 Pass another **trail** to the left that leads to the trail loop. Continue **straight**.

1.7 Carry your bike over the gate and cross **Michigan Avenue**. On the east side of Michigan Avenue, both the canal and the White River are in full view.

2.3 Pass a **trail** on the left.

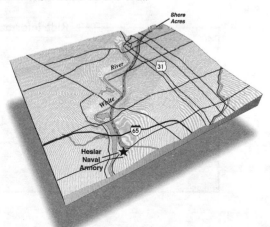

This is another trail that runs parallel to the canal.

2.5   Pass a **bridge** on the right. Cyclists can take this bridge to **Butler University**.

2.8   Pass another **bridge** on the right. Cyclists can take this bridge into **Butler University**. Possible stops include Hinkle Fieldhouse or Holcomb Observatory.

3.0   The **CANAL TOWPATH** crosses **52nd Street**. Continue **straight**. There is a sign here dedicated to the runners who helped raise money for the homeless.

"For generations, the Indianapolis Water Company Canal has hosted thousands of runners, walkers, and bikers along its picturesque banks. Each year, hundreds of runners participate in the annual Turkey Trot run and help feed and clothe the homeless. This plaque is dedicated to those generous runners who have given, so others may have."

3.1   The **CANAL TOWPATH** crosses **53rd Street**. Continue **straight**. Roll past the "Do Not Enter" sign. You are now on a paved, one-way street. This is an access road for the homes that face the canal. Beware of cars in this section.

3.3   Arrive at a paved intersection with a road on the left. Continue **straight** on path.

3.4   Pavement ends and the **CANAL TOWPATH** continues as a singletrack path.

3.5   Pass a singletrack trail to the left. This leads to private property. Stay on the main path.

Ride Information

Trail Maintenance Hotline:
Indianapolis Water Co. Purification Dept.   (317) 923-5073
Schedule:
Open year-round
Track racing:
Major Taylor Velodrome   (317) 327-8356
Maps:
USGS map: Indianapolis, IN

3.6 On the opposite side of the canal is the Butler-Tarkington area. This intersection is not far from the Atlas Supermarket where David Letterman worked as a teenager.

3.8 The trail crosses **Illinois Street**. Continue **straight**.

4.0 The trail crosses **Meridian Street**. Continue **straight**.

4.3 The trail crosses **Kessler Boulevard**. Continue **straight**.

Pennies for the Poet

The tradition of leaving one-cent donations on James Whitcomb Riley's gravesite dates back to when the grave was first built in 1916. The original purpose of the money was to finance the Romanesque-looking monument. Today the money is collected and donated to Riley Children's Hospital. Another interesting fact about Riley's gravesite is that this prime resting spot was awarded to the poet and not the politician. Away from the hill in a less favorable site in Crown Hill Cemetery, the late Hoosier president, Benjamin Harrison, also rests. It just goes to show, politicians don't get all of the best perks—in life or death.

4.7 The trail crosses **Central Avenue**. Continue **straight**. This is where the canal's largest gaggle of geese and flock of ducks reside. If you happen to have a spare loaf of bread in the back pocket of your jersey, consider stopping to feed the waterfowl.

5.0 The trail ends at the **Revco Drugstore** parking lot at the intersection of **63rd Street** and **College Avenue**. But the ride doesn't have to end here. The Village of **Broad Ripple** has many eccentric shops and wonderful eatery's.

11 Whitewater Canal Trail

Ride Specs

Start: Parking area east of Duck Creek Aqueduct

Length: 4.2 of proposed 8 miles

Rating: Easy

Terrain: Flat; grassy canal towpath

Riding Time: 30+ minutes

Other Uses: Metamora, homemade fudge, camping

When young Balser, from Charles Major's *Bears of Blue River*, traipsed around Shelbyville and picked up those notorious bear cubs, chances are he walked along the Whitewater Canal Trail near Brookville.

As he trekked across the eastern portion of the state, he would surely have passed through Metamora. Mrs. John Matson gave Metamora its name, and while she might have known about Balser, she chose to name this town after an Indian princess from a popular New York City play. Metamora was plotted in 1838 with the canal cutting right through the middle of town. This center-line artery contributed to the life, death, and eventual rebirth of the town.

The original glory days were short lived during the river-travel boom that swept the Midwest. After 20 years, river travel was replaced by railroads, and many booming river and canal towns busted. And though a railroad was built directly next to the canal, Metamora still faded into obscurity. Passenger trains eventually stopped traveling along the line, and Highway 52 became the main thoroughfare that connected Indianapolis to Cincinnati, bypassing Metamora altogether.

In the 1940s, new life arrived in the form of local and state funds. They were used to restore the town's aging buildings. 20 years later, craftsmen, boutique owners, and antique dealers settled here and transformed the area into a tourist attraction similar to that of Nashville, Indiana. They began selling their wares and

Metamora's historic Grist Mill.

Getting There

☞ **From Brookville** – Take **Hwy 52 west** approximately 9 miles to **Metamora** and **Pennington Road**. Turn **left** on **Pennington Road** and drive 1 mile to free parking lot east of **Duck Creek Aqueduct**. Pass the shops and Duck Creek Aqueduct before coming to the parking area.

☞ **From downtown Metamora** – Simply follow **Pennington Road east** through town until it ends at the trailhead.

---

created a blossoming economy of crafts, antiques, handmade gifts, and homemade fudge, with the Metamora Grist and Roller Mill as the town's keystone.

This functioning mill was built in 1845 and rebuilt in 1900. Distinguished by its large waterwheel, the mill still uses the canal's water power to pummel the grain. Visitors can purchase a bag of cornmeal and admire the tools of a bygone grain-grinding era.

Another attraction is the 14-ton Ben Franklin barge. Visitors can take a half-hour slow-moving boat tour through the area. Just don't forget to thank the "horse power" (draft horses Rex and Tony) that pulled you along on your tour.

On the way to the trailhead, you will pass the Duck Creek Aqueduct. This 60-foot, water-filled bridge is covered by a wooden shed. Featured in *Ripley's: Believe it or Not*, it is believed to be the only covered bridge aqueduct in existence.

Unique sites aside, the Whitewater Canal is like many rails-to-trails projects across the state. The project is just in its infancy, with only two miles of the trail cut, and should be classified as not yet ready for prime time. The trail is wide and grassy and doesn't see much traffic.

Since the path is wide and flat, cyclists can focus more on the area's surroundings and less on pedaling. In the fall, the colors surrounding Metamora along the rolling hills fill the eyes with wonder. This full-color foliage show has few rivals in the state. In the hues of the dropping leaves, hiding far from the noise of the tourists, cyclists may also spot the elusive great blue heron.

Just past the end of the railroad line, the canal becomes more of a creek. In this back section of the route, hidden in the high brush near the canal's

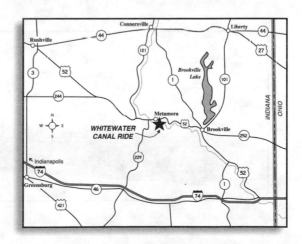

Some of the delightful Hoosier scenery found near the Whitewater Canal Trail.

edge, a blue heron has made a home.

The proposed trail will eventually connect Metamora with Brookville and has the potential of becoming one of the most scenic rail-conversion projects in the state. But judging by the sturdy construction of the gate at the trail's end, it appears it will be some time before the remainder of the trail is opened.

If you would like to help to open the rest of this trail, or help out with other rails-to-trails projects around the state, contact Richard Vonnegut at the Hoosier Rails-to-Trails Council. Yes, he is related to the writer, Kurt Vonnegut. No, he admits that he can't write as well. But Richard is equally passionate about the prospect of cyclists traveling along converted railways throughout the state.

As it stands now, the trail provides a great opportunity to burn off the calories of a delicious fried chicken dinner with all the trimmings from the Hearthstone as well as the delicacies from the homemade fudge shops. In fact, by using Highway 52, a loop can be made from the restaurant, to the trail, and then back again to the homemade fudge shop—a perfect ride!

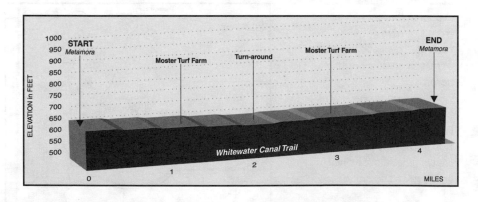

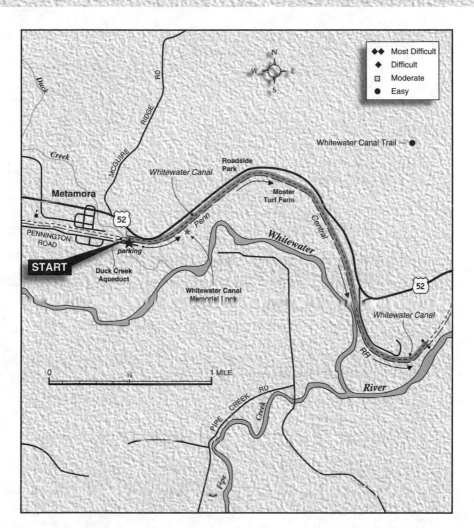

MILES   DIRECTIONS

0.0   **START** at the free **parking area** east
       of **Duck Creek Aqueduct.**
       Leave the parking lot and
       turn **right** on
       PENNINGTON ROAD.

0.05   **PENNINGTON
       ROAD** turns to
       gravel. Continue
       straight.

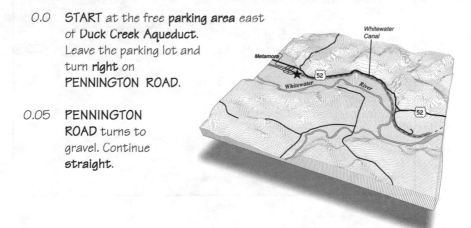

0.1   Pass a **big red barn** and the **"Whitewater Canal Trail"** sign. Continue **straight**, being careful to avoid the electric fence on your right. Now on a wide, grassy canal towpath.

0.5   The **canal towpath** switches to **gravel** and cuts between two fences. The trail crosses a driveway and changes back to a **grassy canal towpath**.

1.2   Cross a gravel driveway leading to the **Moster Turf Farm**. Continue **straight** on the towpath.

1.6   Pass the end of the **train tracks**. Great blue herons nest near this section of the canal.

2.1   Come to the **"Trail Closed"** sign. The **Whitewater Canal Trail** ends here. The remainder of the trail is currently under development. Return to Metamora from which you came.

4.2   Arrive back in **Metamora** for some homemade fudge.

Ride Information

Trail Maintenance Hotline:
Indiana Department of Natural Resources   (317) 232-4070
402 W. Washington
Room 271
Indianapolis, IN 46206-0402

Rails-To-Trails Organizations:
Hoosier Rails-to-Trails Council: (317) 237-9348
P.O. Box 402
Indianapolis, IN 46206-0402

Rails-to-Trails Conservancy   (202) 797-5400
1400 16th Street, NW, Suite 300
Washington, DC 20036-2222

Restaurants:
Hearthstone Restaurant   (317) 647-5204
18149 US Hwy 52
Metamora, IN 47030-9748

Maps:
USGS maps: Metamora, IN; Brookville, IN

Cincinnati — only 52 short miles away!

12 Linton Conservation Club

Ride Specs

Start: Conservation Club parking lot

Length: 1.9 miles of 4-mile system

Rating: Moderate

Terrain: Rolling; reclaimed coalpit ridges and ravines

Riding Time: 25 minutes – 1 hour

Other Uses: Hiking, camping, fishing, square dancing

Before this town became the city of Linton, it was known as the village of Jerusalem. In 1835, a post office was established and the village honored General Linton of Terre Haute by adopting his name.

In 1865 the town's population stood at a mere 200. By the turn of the century, the town had become a coal city and the population grew to 3,100. And during the 1930s, Linton boasted of being the population center of the United States. But as much of the nation moved west, the center of population moved with it and now rests in St. Louis, Missouri. Being the center of the country's population was not taken lightly by Linton, and that era is commemorated by a stone historical marker situated on the trails of the Linton Conservation Club.

As the population moved, so did the industrial focus of Linton. Like many of the trail systems in the southwestern section of the state, the Conservation Club was once a strip mine. Maumee Collieries operated the mine until 1927. After that, the land stood vacant for 17 years until 1942, when its 600 acres were turned over to the city of Linton.

The city worked to reclaim the land by planting trees and stocking fish in the 27 man-made lakes created by the mining company. But after the initial cleanup, for reasons unknown, the land was neglected and improvement projects abandoned.

Getting There

☞ **From Bloomington** – Take **Hwy 45 south** approximately 14 miles to **Hwy 445**. Take **Hwy 445 west** 4 miles to **Hwy 54**. Take **Hwy 54** west approximately 24 miles into **Linton**. Pass the McDonald's and take the next **right** at the **"Sunset Park: Camping and Diving"** sign. This road is **CR 100 West**, but the road sign is blocked. Take **CR 100 West** 0.7 miles to the **Linton Conservation Club**. Turn **right** into the **Conservation Club** and park in front of the **main building**.

Welcome, Cyclists!

In 1993, Jay Gainey read in the local paper that the city council was looking for something to do with this land behind the Conservation Club. Jay then talked with his friend and business partner, Mike Murphy, about the possibility of building a mountain bike park.

In prior years, Jay had searched for places to ride his mountain bike. Though he had jogged on the trails at nearby Shakamak State Park, he believed the park would also be ripe for mountain biking.

These newfound lovers of the sport soon discovered what many cyclists had known for some time. Many of the best trails in the state are off-limits. They rode at the park until the rangers kicked them out.

But Jay and Mike didn't give up; they created their own trails instead. They presented their plan to the Linton City Council for the Conservation Club's land, which had no trails, was overgrown with weeds, and had become an illegal dumping ground. They offered to clean up the dump, cut some trails, and maintain the area with the stipulation that mountain biking be allowed. The city accepted the proposal and the pair went to work immediately.

They spent a week marking trees with ribbons

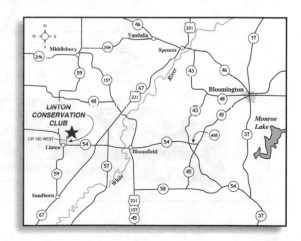

and eyeballing where future trails would be constructed. Jay sought the help and ideas of Norman Gage, Superintendent of City Parks. He explained to Jay the County Corrections Work Program, in which lawbreakers, sentenced to hours of community service, were available for hire.

After the work dates were coordinated, the project was awarded a sizable workforce. On some days as many as 20 men showed up to cut the trails—many of whom brought their own tools.

They worked through the winter and were able to clear four miles of trails in the first season. And with a $1,000 donation from a kickboxing tournament sponsored by Fitness One and American Karate, trail signs were constructed, bridges were built, and a new marquee was placed at the entrance. Now that they have a better understanding of the work involved, Jay and Mike hope to clear seven more miles of trails next year, with the ultimate goal of creating 25 miles of off-road bicycling routes.

> ### Linton Trail Rules
>
> - No motorized vehicles
> - Trails for hiking and biking only
> - Hikers have right of way
> - Bicyclists must stay on trails
> - Bicyclists must wear helmets
> - Hikers and bicyclists must use caution and enter at own risk

The completion of such a circuit will connect the Conservation Club with Sunset Park to the north. Sunset Park offers camping and has both primitive campsites and sites with electrical hookups. The park also boasts of having one of the clearest lakes in the state, offering scuba diving and snorkeling.

Testimony for the trails has come from city officials, race coordinators, and other cyclists. The mayor even showed his support of the trail effort by attending the park's DINO races. Two mountain bike races were hosted by Linton in 1995, and DINO Coordinator Rick Cox called the course one of the top three in the state.

If the first four miles of trails are any indication, the Linton loop is worthy of the praise. The overall topography of the area is flat, with mounds produced from mining activity as the area's only hills. These climbs and descents lack in length but are still technically pleasing. Most of the trails straddle ridges or

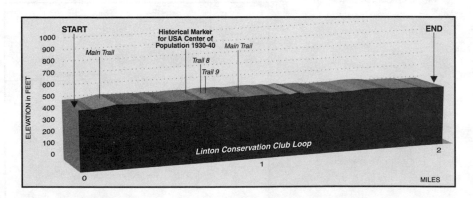

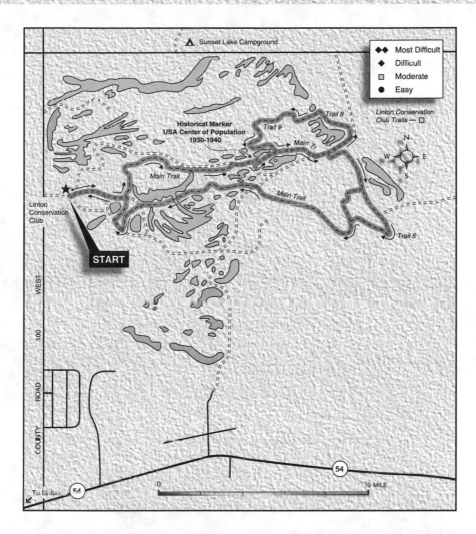

run along the ravines, but two trails serve as the system's roller coaster. A series of whoop-de-doos are found at the ride's halfway point on trails 8 and 9. Here the trail dives from ridge to ravine and back to the ridge. Cyclists have little time to recover from each climb, but enough momentum is gained to carry cyclists through the entire up-and-down run.

If your stomach is not too queasy from Trails 8 and 9, Linton has two favorite nearby eateries. Pizza City fills the bill if the

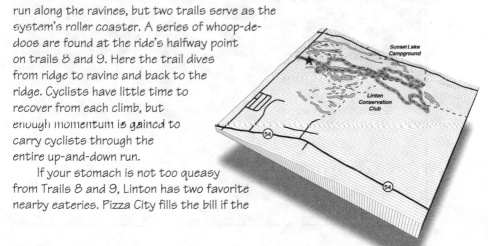

preferred fare is pizza and beer. If a buffet sounds pleasing to the palate, Stoll's Country Inn is a prime choice.

Driving away from Linton, cyclists will have a satisfying feeling that can't be fully credited to the area's food. Riding on an old abandoned coal pit, since transformed by two men into one of the state's best trail systems, truly takes the cake around here.

MILES	DIRECTIONS
0.0	**START** at the **Conservation Club Parking Lot**. Find the trailhead at the **west side** of the **parking lot** on the left side of the trailer. Follow the trail through an open field.
0.05	The trail splits. Take the **left split**.
0.1	Arrive at the **MAIN TRAIL** intersection. There are two signs. Follow the **MAIN TRAIL** to the **left**.
0.2	Arrive at a **trail intersection** with the **"Trail 11"** sign straight ahead. Take a 180-degree turn to the **right**, staying on the MAIN TRAIL.
0.5	The **Main Trail** intersects with a dirt road. Turn **right** on the **DIRT ROAD**.
0.6	Turn **left** off the dirt road onto the **MAIN TRAIL**. Now at the **Historical Marker for the United States Center of Population from 1930-1940**.

Ride Information

Trail Maintenance Hotline:
    Jay Gainey   (812) 847-7682
Camping:
    Sunset Park   (812) 847-8513
        R.R. 2 Box 125A
        Linton, IN 47441
Schedule:
    Linton Conservation Club open year-round, dawn till dusk
Restaurants:
    Stoll's Country Inn   (812) 847-2477
        RT 54 West
        Linton, IN 47441
Maps:
    USGS map: Linton, IN

The author, his truck, and his faithful steed.

0.7   The **Main Trail** intersects with **Trail 8**. Turn **left** on TRAIL 8.

0.71   Atop the first climb, **TRAIL 8** intersects with **Trail 9**. Turn **right** on TRAIL 9. This is the roller-coaster section of the trails. Instead of straddling the ridges, **TRAIL 9** dives up and down, giving riders enough momentum to roll to the top of the upcoming ridge with little effort.

0.8   The trail splits. Take the **left split**.

0.9   Arrive at a **trail intersection** and the "Trail 8" sign. Turn **left**.

0.95   **Trail 8** intersects with the **Main Trail**. Now back at the same point where you started Trail 8. Turn **left** on the MAIN TRAIL.

1.0   The **MAIN TRAIL** intersects with a dirt road. Turn **left** on the DIRT ROAD.

1.05   Follow the "Main Trail" sign and turn **right** onto singletrack.

1.08   Arrive at the intersection of **Trail 5**. Continue **straight** on TRAIL 5.

1.1   **TRAIL 5** splits. Take the **right split** following the "Trail 5" sign and the stack of **four car tires**.

1.3   TRAIL 5 intersects with the **Main Trail**. Turn **left** at the "**Main Trail**" sign.

1.4   The MAIN TRAIL intersects with a dirt road. Continue **straight** on the MAIN TRAIL.

1.5   The MAIN TRAIL intersects with Trail 4. Follow the MAIN TRAIL to the **left**. Immediately arrive at a trail split. Continue to follow the MAIN TRAIL to the **left**.

1.7   The MAIN TRAIL passes **Trails 1,2,** and **3**. Now at an intersection with a dirt road. Continue **straight** on the MAIN TRAIL.

1.8   The MAIN TRAIL intersects with a dirt road. Turn **right** on the DIRT ROAD and follow it back to the **main parking area** or take another lap.

1.9   Arrive at the **Conservation Club Parking Area**. Ride complete.

Wapehani Mtn Bike Park 13

Ride Specs

Start: Wapehani parking lot

Length: 7 miles of trails

Rating: Moderate

Terrain: Hilly; wooded singletrack

Riding Time: 20 minutes – 1 hour

Other Uses: Hiking, jogging, viewing wildlife

Until 1968, Highway 37 was a narrow winding road that made travel difficult even on a good day. Add some foul weather and a dark night, and the road was downright treacherous. But with Bedford attorney and Highway Commissioner Ruel W. Steele at the helm, that would soon change.

Two decades of traveling along the highway from his hometown to the capitol city inspired the commissioner to upgrade the road into a safe, major thoroughfare and connect southern Indiana with Indianapolis.

The state raised funds for the project by placing a two-cent per gallon tax on gasoline, and Highways 37, 31, and 41 were all improved and near completion before Steele's term was complete. He became a hometown hero and received accolades for his political achievement. He was awarded an Indiana University football jersey with the number 37, and years later the highway itself was named after him.

But the widening of the highway brought with it some growing pains. In Bloomington, the widened byway effectively cut Camp Wapehani, a Boy Scout summer camp, in half. Adhering to their motto, the local Boy Scouts were prepared and moved their 30-year-old summer camp to a better location, one farther away from the city with more natural surroundings.

The abandoned Camp Wapehani was given to the city around 1980 and was soon thereafter converted into a mountain bike park, managed by Bloomington Parks and Recreation. Other parks cater to mountain biking, but Wapehani is the only designated mountain bike park in the state.

Getting There

☞ **From downtown Bloomington** – Take **2ⁿᵈ Street** approximately 2 miles to **Weimer Road**. Follow **Weimer Road south** 0.7 miles to the entrance of **Wapehani Mountain Bike Park**. Turn **right** into the park and drive 0.3 miles to the **parking area**.

Cyclists competing in one of the many DINO races held around Indiana throughout the year.

Using only the land east of Highway 37, the trails in Wapehani Park are packed tight. Local mountain bikers designed seven miles of trails in this 35-acre park. And while hikers, joggers, and wildlife enthusiasts are welcome, mountain biking holds the reigns here.

Bloomington Parks and Recreation requires all cyclists to wear helmets, and also encourages cyclists to register and sign a waiver at local bike shops.

The park's design makes it virtually impossible for anyone to get lost in this maze of trails that encircles Wapehani Lake. It is possible, though, to get a great workout without having to ride far from your vehicle. On the map from Bloomington Parks and Recreation there looks to be a simple loop, but this is definitely a create-your-own-loop ride. This spider-web system is a plus for Bloomington-area cyclists who want to put in some rugged miles to

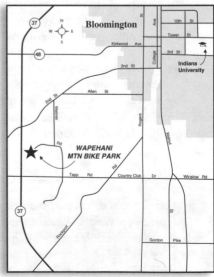

Ride Information

Trail Maintenance Hotline:
Bloomington Parks and Recreation   (812) 349-3700
    349 S. Walnut Street
    Bloomington, IN 47402

Schedule:
Park open from dawn to dusk, year-round

Maps:
USGS map: Bloomington, IN
Bloomington Parks and Recreation trail map

prepare for the Little 500 *(see Little 500 sidebar)*. Few out-of-towners ride this course unless they desire to preview it before the annual DINO mountain bike race *(see DINO sidebar)*.

If you do lose your bearings, use these references: The *grassy field* is on the *north side* of the lake and closest to the parking lot; the *dam* is on the *east side* of the lake; and the *biggest climbs* are on the *south side* of the lake.

DINO Mountain Bike Race Series

DINO (Do INdiana Off-road) is a series of mountain bike races organized by Bloomington-based Crossroads Communications. All of the races are sanctioned by NORBA (National Off-Road Bicycle Association) with the majority of the races held in Indiana. A few other races are hosted by surrounding states.

In 1995, 22 races made up the series with categories from beginner to expert, as well as many age-group categories. There were also four childrens' races for kids 12 and under. The youngsters' races varied from one-half mile to two miles, the entry fee was waived, and all participants received an award.

So, whether you are yearning to become the state champion or you just want to introduce your kids to mountain bike racing, DINO has something to offer you. And with many race courses throughout the state, there is probably a race less than one hour from your home.

For more information, call or write:

Crossroads Communications
P.O. Box 1235
Bloomington, IN 47402
(812) 330-DINO

Little 500

In 1825, Mr. Baynard Hall was, in essence, Indiana University. As the university's sole professor, he taught Greek and Latin to an entire student body consisting of 10 men. Indiana University has since grown to become one of the largest state schools in the country.

Academics aside, Indiana University is most famous for its sporting endeavors. While most Hoosiers revel at the sight of Bobby Knight marching his team to the NCAA Final Four, cyclists pay their homage to the cinders of Bill Armstrong Stadium and the Little 500. Indiana University's annual bicycle race, the Little 500, was created in 1951 and soon grew to become one of the Midwest's most famous bicycle races.

The race is held in April and consists of two separate races, one for men and another for women. Both are contested on the cinder track at Bill Armstrong Stadium; the women race 100 laps and the men race 200 laps. Each field is made up of 33 teams of four riders and two alternates, with the men vying for the William S. Armstrong Championship Trophy and the women competing for the Borg Warner Trophy.

Cyclists race around a quarter-mile running track, but much of the excitement happens in the pits as riders attempt their exchange. The incoming rider races in, dismounts, and throws the bicycle to his teammate. The teammate jumps on the passing bicycle and speeds up to the field of racers. If they're both lucky, they stay upright and avoid sliding across the harsh cinders.

In 1979, the Little 500 was featured in the movie, *Breaking Away*. Actors Dan Stern, Jackie Earle Haley, Dennis Christopher, and Dennis Quaid rode to victory on their cycling team, the Cutters. This movie escalated the Little 500 into the national spotlight, won an Oscar for "Best Original Screenplay," and gave cyclists a cult film that any rider worthy of shaving his legs watches at least once a year. The fame, the bike race, campus dances, ice-cream socials, golf outings, and, of course, the partying has earned the Little 500 weekend the worthy title of "The World's Greatest College Weekend."

Little 500 Facts

- All of the bicycles are donated by the Roadmaster Corporation
- The inaugural race started at 11:00 a.m., just like the Indianapolis 500
- Celebrities such as David Letterman, Bob Hope, the Smothers Brothers, Rich Little, the Jackson Five, and Dionne Warwick have performed at the Little 500—even before *Breaking Away* was filmed
- *Breaking Away* was written by Indiana University alumnus, Steve Tesich, who rode on the winning Little 500 team in 1962

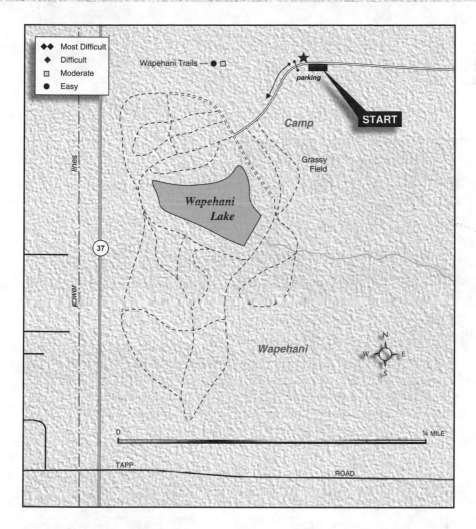

Note: Because Wapehani Mountain Bike Park has so many individual trails suitable for cycling, it would be unreasonable to create a single loop. Instead, cyclists are encouraged to use the map provided as a basic guide into the park, then to create your own loop or just plain ride every trail you see out there. For this reason, there is no profile map available.

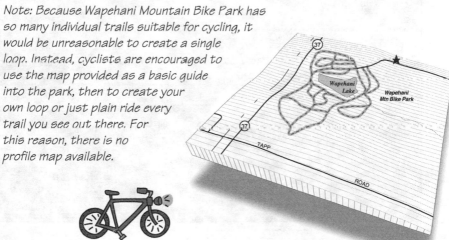

14 Clear Creek Rails-to-Trails

Ride Specs

Start: Clear Creek Parking Area

Length: 3.3 miles of proposed 6.2-mile trail

Rating: Easy

Terrain: Flat; hard-packed dirt path

Riding Time: 40 minutes – 1 hour

Other Uses: Hiking, jogging

The literature provided by the National Rails-to-Trails Conservancy asks cyclists to envision an emerald necklace or a greenway of trails linking America. This is a fine fantasy and one that could be accomplished, but there are some hurdles that must be overcome before it can be completed.

According to Richard Vonnegut, Coordinator for Hoosier Rails-to-Trails, one of the primary stumbling blocks is some very stubborn Hoosier landowners. Some of these residents show ill will because these corridors of land designated for railroads were taken away from them or their ancestors in the first place. The big muscle behind this argument is the Farm Bureau. This large lobbying group has convinced many farmers that this land should be returned to them.

Sights along the rail-trail corridor.

Getting There

☞ **From downtown Bloomington** — Take **College Avenue** south 0.7 miles to **Walnut Street**. Continue south on **Walnut Street** 1.5 miles to **Country Club Road**. Turn **right** on **Country Club Road** and drive 0.2 miles to the **Rails-to-Trails parking area**. Turn **left** at the **"Rails-to-Trails/City of Bloomington Parks and Recreation"** sign.

Another argument states that criminals from bigger cities will use these backways to access private property and be given a quick escape route. Understanding that most crimes happen as a matter of convenience, I don't see too many criminals using a mountain bike as their vehicle of choice.

On the other hand, the arguments for establishing such trailways are numerous. Surveys have shown that more people would ride if safe routes were built. Other supporting arguments include fading business districts that could be revitalized by increasing traffic, a growing number of potential home buyers near such trails, decreased air pollution, and increased health benefits from riding and walking. And with the National Trail Systems Act of 1983 in hand, the Hoosier Rails-to-Trails Council is at the head of these arguments. This law encourages railroad companies to work with communities wishing to convert abandoned lines.

If the Hoosier Rails-to-Trails Council can win this battle, the dream will become a reality. The vision includes abandoned linear corridors converted into useful veins of transportation and miles of flat, well-groomed cycling routes connecting every major city in the state. Some of the paths could be paved, with others surfaced with gravel and perfectly suited for mountain bikes. As land access issues keep some of the best areas closed to cyclists, abandoned rail corridors provide the greatest potential for new trail networks.

There are currently 10 rails-to-trails projects in Indiana. The Clear Creek rails-to-trails is managed by Bloomington Parks and Recreation and is the best rail-trail for mountain bikers in the state. The path originates on the south side of Bloomington and heads southwest out of town. The beginning of the path is covered with pea gravel and later switches to larger gravel and grass.

Once the trail leaves the outskirts of town, the path is predominantly dirt. At a few points, it is bordered by five-foot walls of lime-

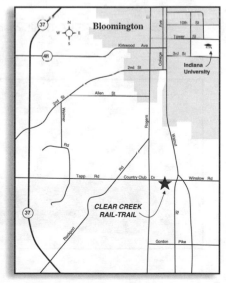

stone, giving it a tunnel effect. When not surrounded by stone, the route is surrounded by hardwood trees.

The trail is mostly flat with the only challenge occurring where a trestle used to be. A quick drop takes cyclists down to the creekbed. The descent is rideable, but you had better check your brakes first, for it drops quickly and offers no ford to cross the small stream. Once at the bottom, shoulder your bike and pick your way across the rocks. The preceding climb is also best undertaken with the bike still on the shoulder.

The trail ends at 3.3 miles and dribbles off into a resident's backyard. Hopefully this is only a temporary end to the trail. The goal is to stretch the trail another three miles to top out at 6.2 miles. There is no gate here and that is a positive sign that the additional three miles will soon be open.

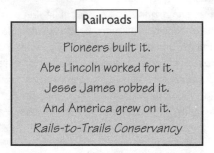

Railroads

Pioneers built it.

Abe Lincoln worked for it.

Jesse James robbed it.

And America grew on it.

Rails-to-Trails Conservancy

MILES   DIRECTIONS

0.0   **START** at the **Clear Creek Parking Area**. Find the trailhead at the **south end** of the **parking area**.

1.0   **CLEAR CREEK TRAIL** crosses **Gordon Pike**. Follow the perimeter of the gravel parking lot to the trailhead.

1.3   **CLEAR CREEK TRAIL** crosses **South Rogers Street**.

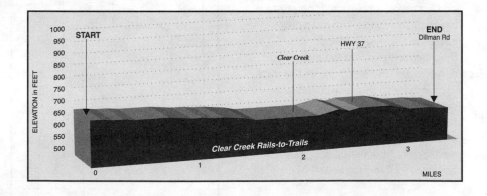

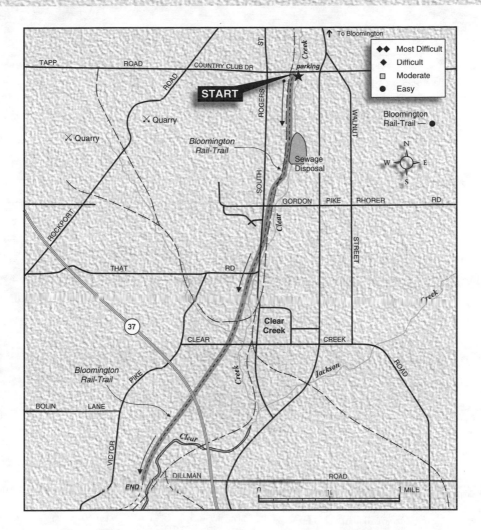

1.5   **CLEAR CREEK TRAIL** crosses **That Road** and skirts the parking lot of **Bloomington Marine and Auto Trim.**

2.0   Come to a creek crossing where a trestle used to be.

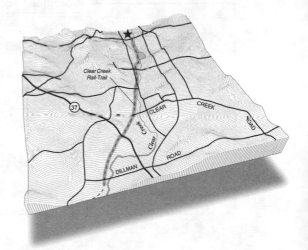

2.1   **CLEAR CREEK TRAIL** crosses a trestle. **CLEAR CREEK TRAIL** splits. Take the **right split**.

2.5   **CLEAR CREEK TRAIL** passes underneath **Hwy 37**.

3.3   **CLEAR CREEK TRAIL** ends at **Dillman Road**. Turn yourself around and head back to the start.

Ride Information

Trail Maintenance Hotline:

Bloomington Parks and Recreation   (812) 349-3700
349 S. Walnut Street
Bloomington, IN 47401

Hoosier Rails-to-Trails Council   (317) 237-9348
P.O. Box 402
Indianapolis, IN 46206-0402

Schedule:

Open from dawn to dusk, year-round

Maps:

USGS maps: Bloomington, IN; Clear Creek, IN

Rails-to-Trails Tidbits

- A storefront area of Dunedin, Florida, was suffering a 35 percent vacancy rate until the Pinellas Trail was established. Now storefront occupancy is at 100 percent and business is thriving.
- In Idaho, parents now feel safe riding bicycles with their children and running errands along the 45-mile Wood River Trail that connects the towns of Bellevue, Hailey, and Sun Valley.
- A household can save up to $3,000 annually by giving up their second car and seeking alternate forms of transportation.
- Missouri's 235-mile Katy Trail traverses nine counties and adjoins 35 towns. Some of these communities have been in decline since the railroad's demise and were initially opposed to the trails, fearing vandals and rowdy trail users. To the contrary, restaurants, pubs, campgrounds, and bicycle rental companies experienced a boom in business. A survey of the trail's western half showed the trail visitors generated an estimated $3 million in local revenue.

ISTEA and Trails: Enhancement Funding For Bicycling and Walking

15 Madison's County Roads

Ride Specs

Start: Rykers Ridge Elementary
Length: 16.8 miles
Rating: Moderate
Terrain: Rolling; paved and gravel county roads
Riding Time: 2 – 2½ hours
Other Activities: Hiking, camping, fossil hunting, bed & breakfasts, antiques

In November, the leaves fall and the hardwood trees go bare, leaving leach-white sycamores looking like mammoth skeletons. The weather throughout most of the winter in Madison, however, remains relatively warm.

The signs around town indicate what's in store for this scenic mountain bike ride. "Visit Historical Madison" is not just an empty tourism promise gauged to fill the bed and breakfasts. Madison is the only city in Indiana, and one of just seven in the country, whose entire downtown area is designated as a historical district.

As a key stop during the booming river transport days, Madison flourished from the 1840s to the 1860s. Once the riverboats were replaced by railroads, the town suddenly became very isolated. Distanced from the main highways and busy railways, the town nearly froze in time. Its economy sputtered during the next hundred years, with few changes made to keep up with the rest of the state.

As you travel through this historically preserved city, sightseeing may seem to take precedence over your intended off-road trek. Along the wide, turn-of-the-century main street you will pass many antique shops, quaint restaurants, and bed and breakfasts (some hosts go as far as greeting guests in period clothing). Several eateries and lodges are housed in the many historic, architecturally diverse buildings.

Getting There

☞ **From downtown Madison** – Take **Jefferson Street** north. Jefferson changes to **Hwy 421.** Take **Hwy 421** 0.6 miles to **Aulenbach Road,** then turn **right.** Turn **left** on **Telegraph** Hill **Road** which later turns into **Rykers Ridge Road.** Take **Rykers Ridge Road north** to **Rykers Ridge Elementary** and **Rykers Ridge Baptist Church.** Park at the school on weekends and park at the church on school days.

Cross this creekbed and stop for the second fossil dig of the ride. Fossils found here can date back nearly 400 million years!

The 1885 Victorian home now known as the Cliff House sits atop the cliffs, overlooking Madison and the murky Ohio River. Many of the upstairs bedrooms offer a great view of the surroundings. Downstairs is a warm parlor and a large breakfast room. In the morning, the table is covered with crois-sants, pastries, fruit, coffee, and juices—the perfect send-off before a lengthy ride.

The area surrounding Madison is blessed with pleasing topography, miles of endless forests, and many challenging hiking trails, but no legal singletrack. Mountain biking is currently not allowed at nearby Clifty Falls State Park or the Jefferson Proving Ground. But cyclists should not fret: just riding on the rolling county roads is an ample workout for even the best cyclists. And as a bonus, there are many historical and scenic stopping points along the way.

One of the first sites that cyclists will pass is the Jacob Ryker home. With his namesake on the ridge, school, and the Baptist church, Jacob Ryker's heritage is marked for many generations to come.

With outcrops of limestone and shale as old as 400 million years, there are numerous places along the ride to search for

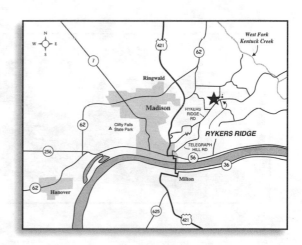

fossils. Take the time to pore over the rocks in search of fossilized spines, shells, and coral from the living creatures of the ancient shallow sea that once covered our land during the Precambrian Period.

Along the creek, the area has a distinctive New England feel. The shallow creek rolls over shelves of limestone and shale as it parallels the road. In the distance waves of evergreens are broken only by a small sheep farm.

The climbs and descents that lace through this scenic country also evoke a mountain setting. There are two major descents on the ride that demand the rider's full attention, especially since they are both surfaced with gravel. The first one, at 4.9 miles, speeds cyclists to a creekbed and the first fossil stop. The second drop comes at the 12-mile mark. To fully enjoy this downhill, take a break at the top of the hill to take in all directions of the view, catch your breath, and check your brakes. Speeds on this 0.3-mile run can reach as high as 40 miles per hour! The gravel and the bend at the creek crossing may unleash an adrenaline rush and a feeling of controlled fear possibly not exhibited since childhood.

Before the next climb, the loop rolls along the flats and beyond a pasture of Belgian horses before splashing through two creek crossings. In the spring, these fords are impassable, not to mention extremely cold.

The last climbs take riders back up to Rykers Ridge and the end of the ride. From here, cyclists can hurry back into town to see if there are any croissants at the Cliff House leftover from breakfast. But if you didn't stay there the night before, the owners might wonder why Lycra-clad individuals are pilfering their food!

MILES DIRECTIONS

0.0 **START** at **Rykers Ridge Elementary School**. Leave the school parking lot, riding **north** on COUNTY ROAD 300 EAST. Ride along the paved road past the **Jacob Ryker house**.

0.5 Turn **left** on COUNTY ROAD 300 NORTH.

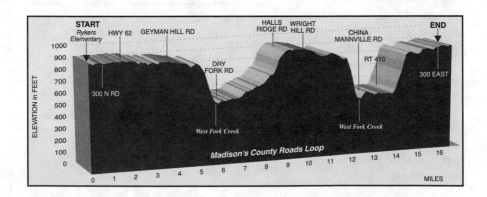

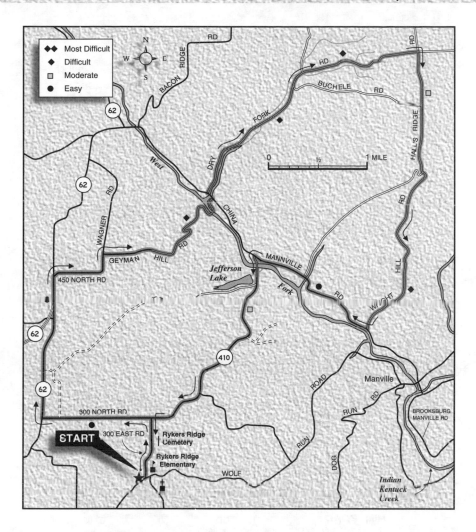

1.7 Turn **right** on **OLD HWY 62**. There is no sign for this paved road.

2.8 Arrive at an intersection. Turn **right** on **HWY 62**. This paved road has a wide shoulder to ride on.

3.9 Arrive at an intersection. Turn **right** on **GEYMAN ROAD**. This paved road turns into **Whippoorwill Road**.

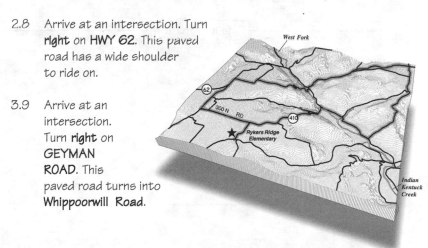

4.5   Pass the **Whippoorwill Girl Scout Camp**.

4.9   The road changes to gravel and descends sharply. **Caution:** there is a sharp turn that can be tricky if traveling too fast on the gravel.

5.6   Cross a low bridge, carrying cyclists across **West Fork Creek**. This is the first **fossil stop**. Take some time to scour the rocks for branch and horn coral, shells, and spines from marine animals of eras past.

5.8   Arrive at an intersection with a paved road. Turn **left** on CHINA/MANNVILLE ROAD.

5.81   Cross **Dry Fork Creek** and take an immediate **right** on DRY FORK ROAD.

5.9   **DRY FORK ROAD** turns to gravel.

6.8   Cross a scenic creek and the second **fossil stop**. If this bridge is out, there is another creek crossing over to the right, within eyesight of this bridge.

8.1   **DRY FORK ROAD** turns back to asphalt and ascends for the day's first major climb.

8.9   Arrive at an intersection with a paved road. Turn **right** on HALL'S RIDGE ROAD.

10.2   Arrive at an intersection with a gravel road. Turn **left** on WRIGHT HILL ROAD.

Ride Information

Where to Stay:
  Cliff House   (812) 265-5272
      122 Fairmount Dr.
      Madison, IN 47250
Places to Hike:
  Clifty Falls State Park   (812) 273-5495
Maps:
  USGS map: Canaan, IN
  Indiana State Road Maps

11.1 Enter the **Wright Hill Wildlife Sanctuary**.

12.0 **WRIGHT HILL ROAD** tops out on a high point with an incredible vista. Prepare for the fastest downhill of the day. **Caution:** the road bends near the end of the descent and crosses a creek.

12.3 **WRIGHT HILL ROAD** intersects with a paved road. Turn **right** on CHINA/MANNVILLE ROAD.

13.9 **CHINA/MANNVILLE ROAD** intersects with a paved road. Turn **left** on **COUNTY ROAD 410 EAST**. There is no sign at this intersection. The road quickly turns to gravel and bends to the left. The right split is a private drive.

14.0 Splash through the **West Fork** creek crossing. These fords are impassable during high water.

14.05 Cross the second creek. The road turns to asphalt and begins the second major ascent.

14.1 The road splits. Stay on **COUNTY ROAD 410 EAST** to the left.

16.2 Arrive at an intersection. Turn **left** on **COUNTY ROAD 300 EAST**.

16.8 Back at **school parking lot**. Ride complete.

16   Lynnville Park

Ride Specs

Start: Main camping area

Length: 2.6 of 6-mile trail system

Rating: Difficult

Terrain: Singletrack; ridges and ravines of reclaimed strip mine

Riding Time: 45 minutes – 1 hour

Other Activities: Hiking, camping, fishing, swimming

Ron Pendley, vice president of the Evansville Bicycle Club, described Lynnville Park best when he added the word "technical" to its title. Mountain bikers interested in challenging, rugged terrain can thank the Peabody Coal Company for this incredibly difficult ride.

The park's ridges and ravines that work the most hard-core cyclists into a frenzy were created from Peabody's now defunct mining operation. After the mine closed in 1964, Peabody donated its 1,100 acres to the nearby city of Lynnville. The once slag heaps are now tree-covered ridges, producing some of the most challenging riding in the area.

The evergreen forest creates somewhat of a misplaced ecosystem giving the trail a slightly western feel. Riding along the ravines while surrounded by evergreens evokes visions of riding in the Rockies—only without the mountain climbs.

Lynnville park has few climbs that are rideable, and most of the descents are very challenging. With the multitude of obstacles, there are few points along the route that allow even one half-mile of continuous riding. This is not the place to introduce a beginner to this sport.

The trail system used to be part of the Black Coal Enduro, one of the most challenging motocross systems on the Enduro circuit. Even straddling a multi-horse engine would not help on some sections of the trail.

The biggest challenges on this trail are the ruts left from ATV wheels and the chunks of limestone lining the trail. Either obstacle can lead to a two-

Getting There

☞ **From Evansville** – Take **I-164 north** approximately 12 miles to I-64. Take **I-64 east** 10 miles to the **Lynnville/Boonville exit (Exit 39)**. Go **north** on Hwy 61 0.1 miles to Hwy 68. Go **west** on Hwy 68 1.5 miles to **Lynnville Park**. Turn **right** into **Lynnville Park** and find a parking spot at the **camping area**.

Even Indiana can get cold. Temperatures on this day reached a balmy 5° above zero. Brrr.....

point takedown into the dirt. The main benefit from riding this system comes from developing bike handling skills similar to those of a "trials rider."

Trials riders show off their skills by riding up and over picnic tables, cars, or log piles, as well as delicately balancing themselves on their front tires with the finesse of an arterial surgeon. Frequent trips through the Lynnville system may raise cyclists' skills close to this level. However, these same challenges might frustrate a less-experienced rider to the point of wanting to sink his bike to the bottom of one of the strip pits.

One highlight of the park is the Wahn Siedler Observatory, sponsored by the Evansville Astronomical Society. The Siedler Observatory has one of the largest telescopes in Indiana. The observatory is far enough from big city lights to afford a detailed view of the stars. Information regarding group reservations and public viewing hours can be obtained by calling the observatory at (812) 922-5681.

Campers have two choices at Lynnville Park: for the social camper, there is the main camp area resembling a subdivision of tents and pop-up trailers; and for those seeking solitude, there are many

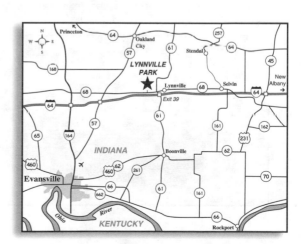

satellite campsites around the lake and near the observatory. Be sure to look for the wild turkeys at these satellite campsites.

Years ago, wild turkeys were eliminated from the state. Far away from the hustle and bustle of the main campground, though, the turkey's amazing comeback can be witnessed as a sizable flock of wild turkeys make their rounds near the sites. If you remain quiet enough, they will wander within camera range and provide the morning's entertainment as you cook breakfast.

One travel tip for campers planning to stay overnight at Lynnville Park is to buy your supplies before you leave your hometown. There is one store in Lynnville, but their prices are pretty lofty. Gas prices are also about 20 cents more per gallon here. *Caveat emptor.*

MILES   DIRECTIONS

0.0   **START** at the **north end** of the **campgrounds**, roll past the bathhouse, and travel **west** on the **GRAVEL ROAD** that cuts between two gravel pits.

0.25   Turn **right** at the sign marked "Rough Road." The trail passes a few lakeside campsites then bends to the right.

0.4   Turn **left** and **cross a bridge**.

0.41   Once across the bridge, take the **faint trail** to the **right**. Follow the ridge overlooking a swamplike overflow from the strip pits.

0.7   Turn **left** on a **DIRT ROAD**.

0.75   Pass a **picnic area** and dive **right** off the dirt road onto a **CREEKBED TRAIL**.

0.8   You now have a choice of three descents off to the right. The middle one looks less intimidating. After this quick descent, most

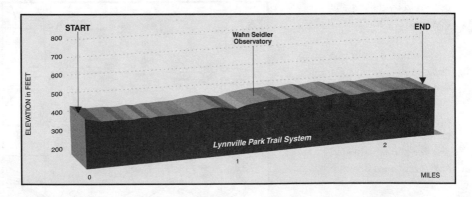

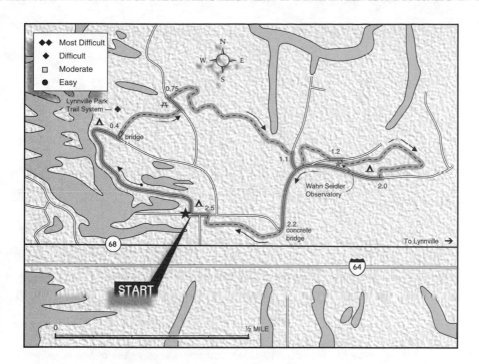

cyclists will have to walk the bike up the following climb.

0.82   Immediately turn **right** at the top of climb.

0.9   Bear **left** at the trail split.

0.95   Turn **left** at top of the trail.

1.0   Come to a faint trail split. Take the **right** split. A short drop puts you between three ridges. Arrive at a challenging descent. Stay close to the center so as to hit the narrow bridge straddling the water and reeds. Now at one of the pit's horseshoe ends.

1.1   Turn **right** on a DIRT ROAD.

1.15   Take a sharp **left** onto another DIRT ROAD and climb to the observatory.

1.2   Turn **left** off the dirt road onto a very **faint trail**. The trail is near the bend in the road, just before the power lines.

1.28   Arrive in the backyard of the **Wahn Seidler Observatory**. Follow the perimeter of the grass yard to the next trailhead nearest the road.

1.47   Turn **left** on the GRAVEL ROAD and ride approximately 100 feet to the trail on the right.

1.5   Turn **right** off the **gravel road** onto SINGLETRACK. Follow the trail to the left.

1.6   Come out of the valley floor and up another sharp, technical climb.

1.7   After the short climb, turn **right** on the WIDE TRAIL. Take an immediate **right**, attempting a steep, technical climb. This is followed by a steep downhill. Now traveling west, parallel to a dirt road.

2.0   Turn **right** on the DIRT ROAD. You are now due east of the observatory. You can take the main dirt road back to your car from here. Head back toward the observatory and follow the road to the left.

2.2   At the next bend in the road, go **straight** toward the **concrete bridge** and follow the SINGLETRACK TRAIL off the road.

2.3   Follow the trail to the **right**. Now traveling parallel to **Hwy 68**, heading toward the entrance of the park.

Ride Information

Trail Maintenance Hotline:
　　Lynnville Park   (812) 922-5144
　　　　Hwy 68
　　　　Lynnville, IN 47619
Watching the Stars:
　　Wahn Seidler Observatory   (812) 922-5681
Schedule:
　　Open from dawn till dusk, year-round
Maps:
　　USGS map: Lynnville, IN

2.5 The trail splits. Take the **right** split just before coming to the entrance road.

2.52 Arrive at a **trail intersection**. Continue **straight**. The trail descends toward the main road.

2.55 Turn **left** on the **MAIN DIRT ROAD** and head back toward the **campground**.

2.6 Ride complete. Now go out and enjoy your own loops and trails in the park!

17 Yellow Banks Recreation Center

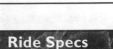

Ride Specs

Start: Big barn in Yellow Banks' parking area

Length: 4.4 of 10-mile trail system

Rating: Moderate

Terrain: Wooded ATV trails and singletrack

Riding Time: 45 minutes – 1 hour

Other Activities: Hiking, swimming

Yellow Banks Recreation Center was founded along the buffalo trace on which wild herds used to travel from grassy meadows to the Ohio River. This path, cut through yellow clay, later served as a route for pioneer travelers.

Today, along that same path and less than a mile outside the town of Selvin sits the recreation area—a mini-resort that offers a multitude of family activities. The Yellow Banks brochure promises an "Escape From Reality." And for only two dollars per carload, Yellow Banks does offer a most impressive list of activities for a day of family fun.

Read these next paragraphs in a single breath using the pitch of a used car salesman to get the full effect of these promos from the recreation center's brochure.

"Swimming! Fishing! Overnight Camping! Pottery Shops! Grocery Store! And much, much more! Relax and tan on the huge sand beach! Including diving, trapeze, and playground (lifeguards on duty)!

"Picnic under the cool shelter houses! Enjoy a game of horseshoes or volleyball! Or bring your bicycle for a peaceful ride on the bicycle trails!

"Cool off with homemade ice cream made daily at Yellow Banks Grocery Store and Bait!" Let's just hope they don't confuse the groceries and the bait when churning the ice cream.

Getting There

☞ **From Evansville** – Take I-164 approximately 12 miles to I-64. Take I-64 **east** 10 miles to the Lynnville/Boonville exit (Exit 39). Go **north** on Hwy 61. Go 0.1 miles to Hwy 68. Go **east** on Hwy 68 10.9 miles to Selvin. Go **north** on **East 700 Road,** marked by the **Yellow Banks Recreation Center** sign. Go approximately 0.7 miles to the **Yellow Banks Recreation Center entrance.** Turn **left** into the park and follow the **Park Entrance Road** to the **parking area.**

"Facilities include restrooms, hot showers, electric and sewer hookups, water, and picnic tables! Cabins now available to rent! Holiday World only minutes away!

"Events include the famous Yellow Banks Craft Show! Second and third weekends in September! Featuring hundreds of booths, pony rides, buggy rides, antique machinery at work, live music, breakfast, corn bread, BBQ, and bean soup! Flea markets!" Wow!

One word of caution, though. The brochure also warns patrons to beware of "thrown clay." It appears that this happens frequently near the Pottery Shop. Cautiously watch as artisans shape flower pots, dinnerware, and jack-o'-lanterns from Yellow Banks' clay. Understand that neither Yellow Banks nor the publisher of this book will assume any liability as a result of injuries sustained from thrown clay.

Now that you've had an aerobic workout from reading the promos, and assuming that you haven't been struck by flying clay, you're warmed up and ready to ride the trails.

Originally, the trails were open to lot owners who had motorcycles and ATVs. But as that trend passed, the owner decided to expand his operation and open the trails to mountain biking. Although the trails were cut by motorized bikes, the owner has reduced the number of permits offered to motorcycle riders with the hopes that mountain biking will become the mainstay.

Yellow Banks is a moderate trail system that is in somewhat of an infant stage. The route is enjoyable to ride, but there are a few confusing sections in which a number of trails intersect. Even a map may not be of great assistance. On a positive note, if you do lose the exact route that was mapped, keep heading in the same general direction and

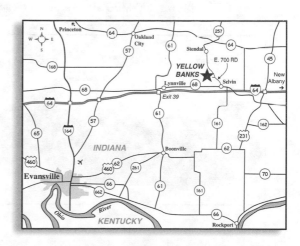

you will come across the trail loop a little farther along.

The confusing portions of the trail are a result of ATVs cutting too many trails in a small area. There is a clearly visible keynote marker at each of these sections, though, that should indicate that you are heading in the right direction.

The climbs at Yellow Banks are not overly difficult and the trail is predominantly singletrack. There are a few swampy sections, but these seem to be isolated.

Note: Because Yellow Banks Recreation Area has become such a labyrinth of trails from heavy ATV use, it would be unreasonable to consider accurately mapping every trail in the system. Instead, both author and publisher have attempted to show that a loop through this network of crisscrossing trails is possible, but that detailed directions for this particular loop would require an unbearable amount of labeling for all of the many twists and turns involved. Cyclists are encouraged to use the forest map provided and to follow both the SIMBC (Southern Indiana Mountain Bike Club—now defunct) and DINO (Do INdiana Off-road) arrows and trail markings to help guide them through this sometimes crazy, but always fun network of off-road bicycling trails. For this reason, there are no detailed mile-by-mile directions available. However, keynote directions and a profile map of the connecting trails making up this loop are provided for useful trail and terrain references. Have fun and try not to get too lost!

MILES DIRECTIONS

0.0   **START** from the trailhead at the **south end** of the **parking lot.** Look for the **GRASSY TRAIL** below the **dam.**

0.2   Arrive at a **trail intersection.** Take the **SIMBC** (Southern Indiana Mountain Bike Club) **TRAIL** to the **left.**

0.5   Follow the **SIMBC** sign and trail to the **left.**

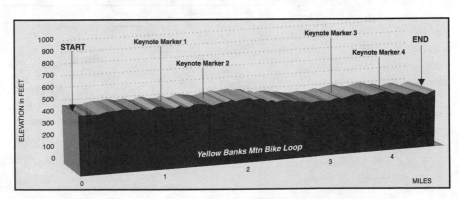

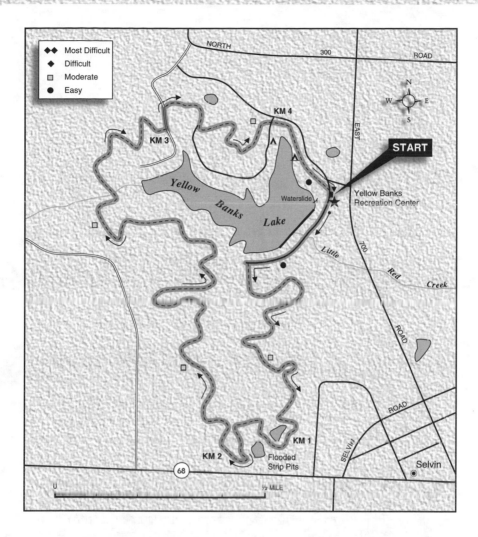

KEYNOTE MARKER 1

1.1 Trail arrives at a "T." Turn **left.** Now at an open area close to a **strip pit.**

1.2 Arrive at a "T." Stay on the trail that follows the perimeter of the pit.

1.3 Follow the trail leading through the two strip pits.

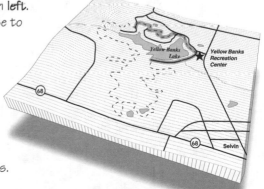

Ride Information

Trail Maintenance Hotline:
Yellow Banks Recreation Center   (812) 567-4703
    RR 2 Box 160
    Dale, IN 47523

Costs:
Mountain Biking is free; $1.50 per person to swim and to use showers, $2 per carload

Schedule:
Open from dawn till dusk, year-round

Maps:
USGS map: Holland, IN

1.4   Turn **left** on the farthestmost right trail and begin your first climb of the ride.

1.5   Arrive at a **trail intersection**. Turn **left** and descend toward the pits.

KEYNOTE MARKER 2

1.6   At the end of a quick descent, look for a small trail to the right. Dive off the main trail to the smaller trail. Now entering a confusing section of unmarked trails. Many ATVs continue to cut new trails, constantly changing the system's layout.

KEYNOTE MARKER 3

3.2   Trail arrives at a "T" at a gravel road. Turn **left** on the GRAVEL ROAD.

3.9   Arrive at a **trail intersection**. Continue **straight**. Pass a house on your right.

KEYNOTE MARKER 4

3.91 The trail crosses a paved road. Continue **straight** on the trail.

4.0   The trail splits soon after it crosses the road. Take the **left split**.

4.4   The trail ends at the **Recreation Center**.

18 Gnaw Bone Camp

Ride Specs

Start: Gnaw Bone Camp main lodge

Length: 7.4 of 25-mile trail system

Rating: Moderate

Terrain: Hilly; singletrack

Riding Time: 45 minutes – 2 hour

Other Activities: Hiking, lodging, cross-country skiing

For many years, the Gnaw Bone trails defined Hoosier mountain biking. Area cyclists knew this 1,560-acre camp to be one of only a few legal and challenging places to ride—and for the most part, they were right.

But even with many new legal trail systems opening to cyclists each year, Gnaw Bone Camp will likely always rank as one of the state's better systems. It is also the award winner for having the most unique name. In typical Hoosier fashion, there is a tale for how the town earned its moniker.

A local sheep farmer was having trouble with the onslaught of wild dogs regularly raiding his herd and feeding on his sheep. With no other solutions in sight, the farmer killed all the sheep, and his family feasted on mutton. A local storyteller sat at the grocery store and told all who would listen that "they have been gnawing sheep bones over at Sally's all summer."

On arrival at Gnaw Bone Camp, your first course of action, like it or not, will be to pet the pack of golden retrievers suddenly surrounding your vehicle. The hounds can get fairly feisty if you ignore their request. Also set aside some time to talk with Alice Lorenz, part owner/caretaker of the camp. Alice asks that you call (812-988-4852) before showing up to ride since she does not open the camp when the trails are muddy.

Alice will tell you that her father, Fred Lorenz, spent much of his life in Indianapolis as an industrial arts teacher at Country Orchard Day School. In 1944, he took the first step to fulfilling his lifelong dream of running his own camp. He bought a substantial plot of land in Brown County and eventually accumulated over 1,560 acres. He claims that the first 1,000 acres cost substantially less than the last 560 acres because of the increased interest

Getting There

☞ **From Columbus** – Take **Hwy 46 west** approximately 13 miles to **Hwy 135 south**. Take **Hwy 135 south** 1.9 miles to **Gnaw Bone Camp**. Turn left into **Gnaw Bone**. Park at the **general store**.

in Brown County property.

Alice's father allowed Boy Scouts and other campers to enjoy their land, and in 1943 the Lorenzes sponsored their own summer camp. These two-week sessions were open to both boys and girls, but recently they've switched to all-girl sessions.

In 1993, Gnaw Bone's summer camp celebrated its fiftieth anniversary with 500 camp alumni attending the party to swap campfire stories and drink Gnaw Bone's legendary beverage—sassafras tea. Campers claim the tea is less than tasty, but since it is the product of Gnaw Bone's very own sassafras trees, sipping this drink stirs fond memories.

With stories out of the way, it's time to enjoy a memorable ride. After signing in for your ride and paying the $2.50 trail fee, pick up a map detailing the 25-mile trail system, and take the north trail from the parking lot. The first climb rolls up Haunted House Road and past the eloquent "Gnaw Bone Hilton," which is merely a screened-in cabin. At the top of the climb, take Lookout Cabin Trail for a short distance to Copperhead Ridge. This becomes a walk-only section when crossing paths with hikers or ATV riders.

Roll along Raspberry Ridge to the Downey Trail

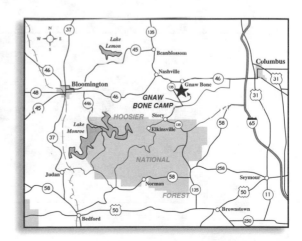

and check out the Lorenz's hilltop spread. Sitting majestically atop a high clearing, the house enjoys one of the most breathtaking views in Gnaw Bone.

After passing the estate, cyclists soon come upon the most technical sections of the trail system. A steep twisting descent bottoms out at a creekbed, bringing cyclists to the low point of the area's topography. That can mean only one thing—the trail must ascend. These climbs are rideable, assuming you are a techno-master with large anaerobic capacity and durable legs.

On the backside of the property, hardwood forest gives way to magical evergreen woods. Ferns, moss-covered logs, and a canopy of pine needles reveal a surreal scene. As you wind through the fairy-tale forest, the trees break and the woods turn to pasture. A mural-inspiring scene unfolds as the backdrop of a forested ridge accents the waving pasture grass that surrounds an aging pole barn.

As the trail turns south, you will break back toward the main lodge and enter the hardwood forest again. Here you will find the historic cabin of Chief Eaglefeather. Consider taking a short rest here because the next climb requires fairly strong legs. For every climb, though, there is an equally rewarding descent, and the following hill takes you all the way back to the main lodge.

After the ride, if you choose to stay, you have the option of playing checkers on tabletop boards or watching the hummingbirds fight for the feeder. If you relax on the homemade furniture of the covered porch long enough, you might even spot a blue-tailed skink. And don't forget to ask Alice about Gnaw Bone and its fantastic past.

MILES   DIRECTIONS

0.0   Take the trailhead at the north end of the parking lot. Walk across footbridge and head **north** on HAUNTED HOUSE TRAIL.

0.4   Peel off the creek bed and turn **left** up the HAUNTED HOUSE TRAIL climb.

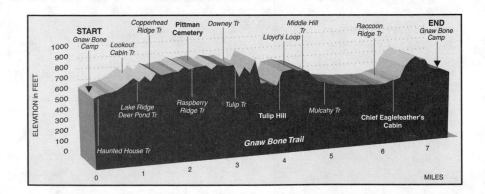

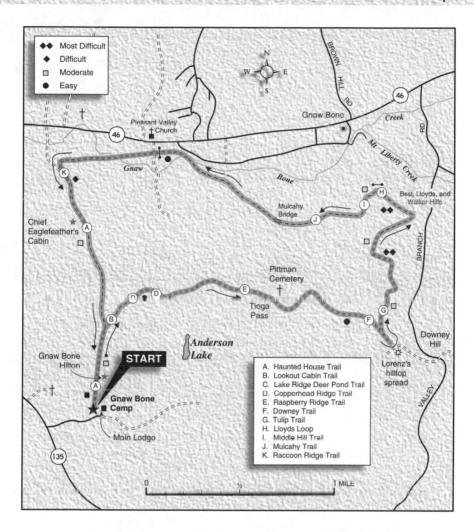

Legend

- ◆◆ Most Difficult
- ◆ Difficult
- ☐ Moderate
- ● Easy

A. Haunted House Trail
B. Lookout Cabin Trail
C. Lake Ridge Deer Pond Trail
D. Copperhead Ridge Trail
E. Raspberry Ridge Trail
F. Downey Trail
G. Tulip Trail
H. Lloyds Loop
I. Middle Hill Trail
J. Mulcahy Trail
K. Raccoon Ridge Trail

0.6   The trail splits at the top of the hill. Take the **right** split.

0.7   Follow the **LOOKOUT CABIN TRAIL** that splits off to the **right**.

0.8   The **LOOKOUT CABIN TRAIL** splits. Take the **LAKE RIDGE DEER POND TRAIL** to the **right**.

1.3   Bear **left**, following the **COPPER-HEAD RIDGE TRAIL**. This is an easement trail that crosses the

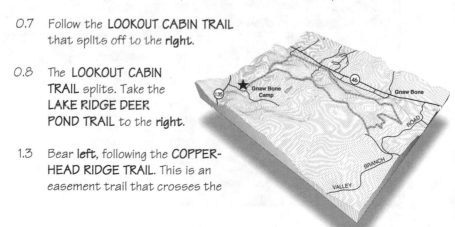

neighbor's property. Stay on the trail and walk your
bikes if you come upon hikers or ATV riders.

1.7   Arrive at a **trail intersection**. Take the **left** trail.

1.9   Roll past **Tioga Pass**.

2.2   The trail becomes **RASPBERRY RIDGE**. Here, cyclists can turn
        right down Cemetery Hill and visit the graves dating back to the
        1850s at **Pittman Cemetery**.

2.6   The trail splits then comes back together again. Immediately after
        the trail comes together, take the **left** split. Roll past a couple of
        logging trails.

2.9   Arrive at the **Tulip Trail/Downey Trail** split. Turn **right** and follow
        DOWNEY TRAIL.

3.1   The trail empties into an open field where you can see the incred-
        ible house built by Alice's father. You are still on Gnaw Bone
        property here. Return to **DOWNEY TRAIL**.

3.3   Bear **right** on **TULIP TRAIL** at the southeast corner of Gnaw Bone
        property. Big chainring time.

3.7   Technical riders rejoice as the trail leads to the steepest and
        most challenging descents and ascents. Take a **left** at **Walkers
        Hill** and descend rapidly. Follow an unnamed creekbed trail past
        Best Hill and **Lloyd's Hill**.

Ride Information

Trail Maintenance Hotline:
    Gnaw Bone Camp   (812) 988-4852
        1888 S. State Rd. 135
        Nashville, IN 47448-9056
Costs:
    $2.50 per person; Call first to find out if the trails are open
Schedule:
    Open from dawn till dusk
Maps:
    USGS map: Nashville, IN
    Gnaw Bone Camp trail map, available at Gnaw Bone Camp

4.0 Arrive at a **trail intersection**. Take a **left** up **Tulip Hill**. Shift as you turn on the trail to prepare for 145 foot climb. If you want to focus on technical riding only, riders can create a loop on this northeast section of the property.

4.3 The trail splits. Take the **right** split along **LLOYD'S LOOP**. Soon after, follow the trail to the **left** and pass the gate on your right.

4.4 Bear to the **left**. Now at the top of the climb.

4.6 Veer **right** onto **MIDDLE HILL TRAIL**. Do not go left. The left trail takes you off Gnaw Bone property.

4.9 Arrive at a **trail intersection**. Turn **right** onto **MULCAHY TRAIL**.

5.0 Arrive at a **trail intersection**. Turn **left**. This is one of the few places in Indiana where you can ride through waist-high grass and not feel the sting of nettles. You might pick up a few chiggers, but that's another story.

5.7 Cross **Mulcahy Bridge**. Follow the trail along the northern perimeter of the camp.

5.9 Go through the gate. Please close the gate behind you, it keeps the horses in their pasture. Now riding across a picturesque field.

6.3 Pass a barn, cross **Gnaw Bone Creek**, then pedal into another field. Turn **left** up **RACCOON RIDGE TRAIL**.

6.4 Arrive at a **trail intersection**. Go **straight** and turn off **Raccoon Ridge Trail**. Follow the **unmarked trail** to the right around the barn.

6.6 Pass **Chief Eaglefeather's cabin**. Technical climb ahead.

7.0 Arrive at a **trail intersection**. Turn **right** onto **HAUNTED HOUSE TRAIL**.

7.1 Bear **left** at the split. This is a wide logging road. Big chain ring all the way to the bottom.

7.4 Turn **right** out of the field and into a creek bed. Follow the trail back to the parking lot. Watch out for the dogs!

Hoosier National Forest

In the 1930s, southern Indiana farmers were in a dilemma. Their land was marginally productive at best, and the markets where they could sell their crops were miles away. Low crop prices, several droughts, and the Depression aggravated farmers' efforts and prompted many of them to leave their homesteads in search of a better life.

These delinquent properties in turn created a concern with state legislators. Indiana's governor Paul McNutt asked the Forest Service to convert these abandoned farms into a national forest. His request was approved, and in 1935, Indiana bought the first parcels of land that would be called the Hoosier National Forest.

Over the next few decades, more land was bought with the immediate goal being to control erosion and wild fires. Manpower for many of the projects was provided by the Civilian Conservation Corps. These unemployed workers not only rehabilitated much of the damaged and abandoned land by reforesting, but they also helped develop many of Hoosier National Forest's recreation areas.

Today, the Hoosier National Forest spans over 193,000 acres, with trails running from Bloomington to the Ohio River. With state parks drawing much of the weekend traffic, the forest trail areas enjoy less congestion, lower costs, and sites that perhaps only a relative few Hoosiers have seen. With regards to mountain biking, the forest is truly the Graceland of Indiana off-road bicycle riding.

Seemingly endless miles of trails serve to entertain cyclists of all abilities. For beginners, or cyclists wanting to spend more time watching wildlife, Tipsaw Lake, Birdseye, or the Oriole Trail are fulfilling options. For hard-core cyclists anxious to spend hours grinding granny gears or scrubbing brake pads down to metal, Youngs Creek, Knobstone, and Hickory Ridge serve up more challenging rides. Ability aside, cyclists can find short loops or all-day rides at many locations in Hoosier National Forest.

Cyclists would be remiss if they came to the forest only to ride, though. At the developed recreation areas, fishing, boating, hiking, and viewing wildlife are only a handful of activities that can be enjoyed. As an added bonus, camping is free on the majority of the forest's property.

In the near future, more mountain bike trails will be opened. In fact, forest officials are always looking for individuals or groups to volunteer for trail improvement or trail construction projects. Imagine the fulfillment of riding on a trail that you helped construct. For more information on volunteer projects, call one of the Hoosier National Forest Offices.

In the meantime, tread softly and enjoy some of the finest trails Indiana has to offer.

Knobstone Trail 19

Ride Specs

Start: Parking area off Elkinsville Rd

Length: 17 miles; 8.5 miles one way

Rating: Difficult

Terrain: Hilly; wooded singletrack

Riding Time: 2½ hours total

Other Activities: Hiking, horseback riding, viewing wildlife

For many mountain bikers, Nebo Ridge defined Hoosier National Forest's 193,036 acres. Historically, this area has always been one of the most popular off-road bicycling locales, but its only legal mountain bike trail, the Knobstone Trail, was rarely the only path followed.

At many intersections you will see U.S. Forest markers branching in multiple directions. The Knobstone Trail is part of the much larger Nebo Ridge system, with the majority of Nebo Ridge's paths dedicated solely to hikers. In fact, one section is being designated strictly as a rare vegetation area. More trails should be open soon here, but the out-and-back Knobstone route is currently this area's only choice for mountain bikers.

Seemingly endless miles of hardwood forest surround the trail on all sides, and the forest's distinctive layers are visible from every angle. Here cyclists can envision what much of state looked like during the frontier days.

The forest's canopy acts as a thick umbrella shielding much of the ground from the sun. The large trees steal sunlight from the next layer of smaller trees and shrubs called the "understory." These plants then act as a subcanopy for the forest floor. Here, leaves, sticks, and fallen trees decompose, leaving mosses, ferns, wildflowers, and mushrooms to flourish.

At the trailhead, the closest town is Elkinsville, which, during the

Getting There

☞ **From Columbus** – Travel **west** on Hwy **46** for 13 miles to Hwy **135 south**. Take Hwy **135 south** 9 miles to **Story**. Veer off Hwy **135** at the **Story Inn** (this is **Elkinsville Road**, but it is unmarked). Travel 2.7 miles and pass a gravel road on your right. Take the **left bend** in the road and cross a **bridge**. Go 0.4 miles, then take a **left** into the **parking area**. This parking area is little more than a widened forest road.

1850s, was quite a trading hub. Today, though, Elkinsville is better known as a town that was bought out by government. When plans were made to flood the area for Monroe Reservoir, the town was purchased by the state and most of the residents moved away. A cluster of houses still remains in the area, as do some ill feelings toward the buyout and government intervention.

Residents have even gone as far as placing a fence across the county road that leads to one of Nebo Ridge's old trailheads. Rangers hesitate to intervene and the town is isolated enough that county officials tend to ignore that the fence has been built. So cyclists beware.

For the most part, the Knobstone Trail follows the ridgetops. There are a few climbs, but all are within reason and are rideable for intermediate cyclists. Since this trail takes you nine miles away from your vehicle, it's a good idea to carry tools, plenty of food and water, and additional layers of clothing.

One of the area's highlights, though not yet open to mountain biking, is Browning Mountain. This ridgetop features several rectangular-shaped slabs of limestone. The spectacular view from these stone benches conjures up images of the Appalachian mountains to the east. With pockets of steam dividing the layers of distant ridges, climbing up to view the "Little Smokies" is definitely worth the hike.

In typical Hoosier fashion, many tales have been spun over the origin of the stones. One such story explains that Native Americans dragged the stones from the lowlands and built a castle on the hilltop. Today many Native Americans still make annual pilgrimages to worship on the hilltop.

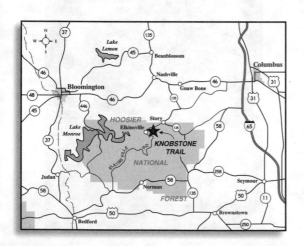

Another tale has it that a farmer piled the stones away from his farmland in order to clear a field. The geological explanation seems most likely, though. Water from an ancient sea exposed the rock and shaped it over the years, and as the water receded, the stones were left piled on the hilltop.

Away from the stony

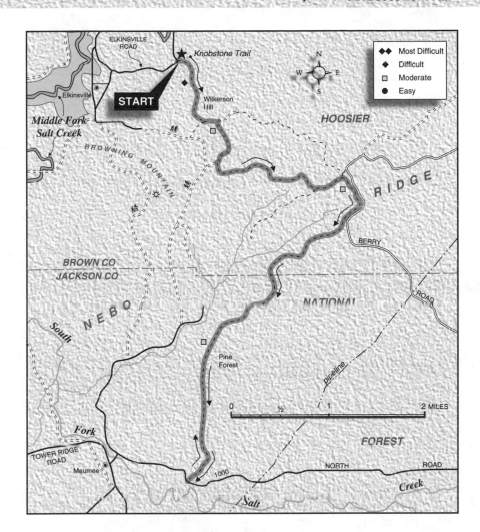

scenic hilltop, a soothing refuge awaits. The perfect finale for this ride is a weekend stay at the Story Inn, where you will be welcomed by Small, an adopted stray taken in by the Story Inn. The inn features hot showers, antique-decorated rooms, and a variety of gourmet meals— all within three miles of the trailhead. Who says mountain bikers don't like to be pampered?

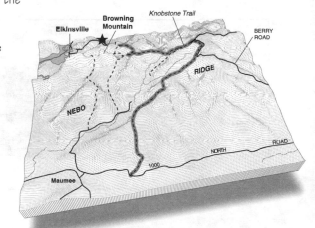

MILES   DIRECTIONS

0.0   **START** from the **gravel trailhead** at the end of the **parking area.**

0.5   Arrive at a **trail intersection.** Follow the **main trail** straight across.

0.6   **KNOBSTONE TRAIL** widens from singletrack to doubletrack.

0.8   **KNOBSTONE TRAIL** splits. Follow the trail to the **left.** The U.S. Forest Service is currently deciding if they want to open the other section on the right to mountain biking.

1.0   A small trail splits off to the left. Stay on the main **KNOBSTONE TRAIL** to the **right.**

1.5   **KNOBSTONE TRAIL** splits to the **left** and changes from doubletrack back to singletrack.

3.9   **KNOBSTONE TRAIL** runs parallel to the gravel **Berry Road.**

4.2   Arrive at a **trail intersection.** Continue **straight.**

7.1   Enter the **pine forest. KNOBSTONE TRAIL** becomes covered in a carpet of pine needles.

7.3   **KNOBSTONE TRAIL** splits. Take the **left** split.

8.5   **KNOBSTONE TRAIL** ends at **County Road 1000 North.** Turn around and head back to the start. Hope you brought some food with you!

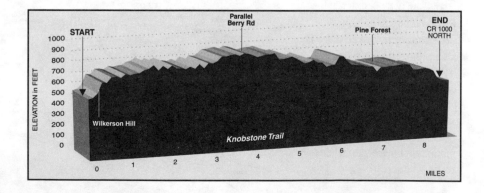

Ride Information

Trail Maintenance Hotline:
Hoosier National Forest   (812) 275-5987
    811 Constitution Ave.
    Bedford, IN 47421
Brownstown Ranger District   (812) 358-2675
    608 West Commerce St.
    Brownstown, IN 47220

Group Rides:
Sundays at 12:00 p.m.   (812) 339-3457
    Bicycle Garage
    507 E. Kirkwood
    Bloomington, IN 47408

Mountain Bike Tours:
Trails Unlimited, Inc. Tours   (812) 988-6232
    RR 4, Box 318
    Nashville, IN 47448
Cost: $40 per person, includes lunch at the Story Inn

Accommodations:
Story Inn   (812) 988-2273
    6404 S. State Rd 135
    Nashville, IN 47448

Maps:
    USGS maps: Story, IN; Elkinsville, IN

20 Hickory Ridge Recreation Area

Ride Specs

Start: Campground parking area

Length: 6 miles of 43-mile system

Rating: Moderate

Terrain: Hilly; wooded singletrack and forest roads

Riding Time: 45 minutes – 2½ hours

Other Activities: Hiking, horseback riding, camping

Early settlers first viewed these large tracts of forest as an obstacle to their progress, and soon clear-cut much of it to make way for farmland. From 1870 to 1910, sawmills harvested much of the vast forest that blanketed a large part of the state, tearing down black walnut, tulip poplar, black cherry, and white oak. The remaining cull trees were deemed useless and were cut and burned.

The Depression forced many farmers to abandon their property, causing a concern among officials over the growing number of delinquent homesteads. In 1934, Governor Paul McNutt approached the Forest Service to buy this land and set it aside as a national forest.

They accepted his proposal and the initial plots were purchased one year later. To replenish the barren ground, the Civilian Conservation Corp was brought in. These unemployed workers began reforesting and controlling the massive erosion problems. In fact, over the next seven years, the Conservation Corp was a major work force behind many of the Hoosier National Forest projects, and since then the base has expanded considerably.

The result is that thousands of wooded acres are being preserved and portions of Indiana returned to a pristine state, a reminder of a time when pioneers first crossed our borders.

Getting There

☞ **From Bloomington** – Take Hwy 446 south approximately 33 miles to Hwy 58. Go **east** on Hwy 58 approximately 7½ miles through **Norman Station** to County Road 1250 west. Look for the **Hickory Ridge** sign on your right. Go **north** on County Road 1250 west. County Road 1250 west turns into **Route 650 north**. At 0.2 miles, the road splits and turns to gravel. Take the right split following the small **U.S. Forest Service** sign. At 0.7 miles turn **left** into **Hickory Ridge's** parking/camping area.

Around Hickory Ridge, acres of wooded hills cover and surround outcrops of limestone. And as Indiana writer Scott Russell Sanders discovered in this area of southern Indiana, limestone is a topic that can break the glare of any stony-eyed local and quickly change terse responses into hour-long amblings.

For his book, *Stone Country*, Sanders interviewed many stone men and passed on the collective passion inspired from the limestone that dominates the landscape of the southern third of Indiana.

"I am glad to live in this pocket of rumpled hills where the crust of the earth shows through. When the fog of human voices grows too thick for my lungs, and the ticking of my own inner clock rattles my soul, and I feel the winds of momentariness whistling through my ribs, I go out to climb a cliff or splash down a stony creekbed or dangle my legs over a quarry's lip."

Sanders, also a cyclist, may have edited out the line, "...or climb the leg-breaking hills carved from glaciers that crumpled the land and the limestone beneath." If Sanders ever needed inspiration to write *Mountain Bike Country*, I would introduce him to Hickory Ridge.

Hickory Ridge holds the largest expanse of mountain bike trails in the state. In this 43-mile system, there are several loops from which

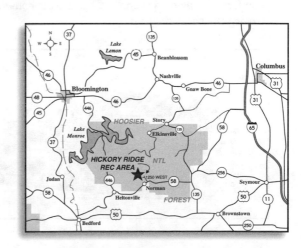

to choose. Each intersection of this system has trail signs, and the distances between the markers, based on the Hoosier National Forest maps, are accurate. It is easy to gauge fitness by choosing a distance and a trail that matches your skill.

Whatever trail you choose, or however long you plan to ride, you may be hard pressed to ride all of these trails in a single weekend. With the focus at Hickory Ridge being hiking, horseback riding, and mountain biking, there are few other amenities or activities offered at this recreation area. This combination may appeal to hard-core cyclists who want to combine two full days of riding seemingly endless trails with some primitive backcountry camping.

One bit of advice: whenever tackling these longer, backwoods routes, it's best to carry tools, spare tubes, and plenty of food and water. And with the fickle weather often found in Indiana, be sure to carry a few extra layers of clothing.

With the variety of loops, ride times can vary from 45 minutes to all day long. Examine the map in this book to see which loop you want to tackle. The routes in the northeast section are the most moderate. The trails follow the land's contours with ridable descents and ascents.

The trails in the northwest sections, though, are a bit more challenging. Instead of following the contours, these routes climb and descend the area's hills and valleys. But as a reward, these paths lead cyclists to the observation tower.

Here, on the backside of the property, just off Tower Ridge Road, stands the tower. Climb to the top and preview the land you're about to ride, or gaze at the hills you've already climbed. To fully appreciate the view, take a pair of binoculars. During the summer, turkey vultures and hawks can be seen circling above the treetops.

The tower isn't the only place to spot wild birds, though. Along the trail, grouse are sometimes stirred and will run as fast as cyclists can ride. They will run to a clearing, then break into flight.

Another interesting novelty of the grounds is its facilities. "His" and "Hers" outhouses in the parking area/campground provide ample backwoods comfort, and also squelch that age-old outhouse argument that spawns from leaving the toilet seat up!

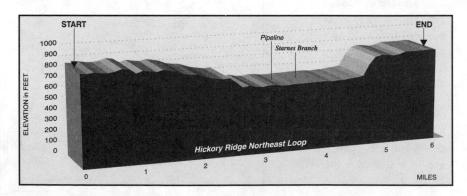

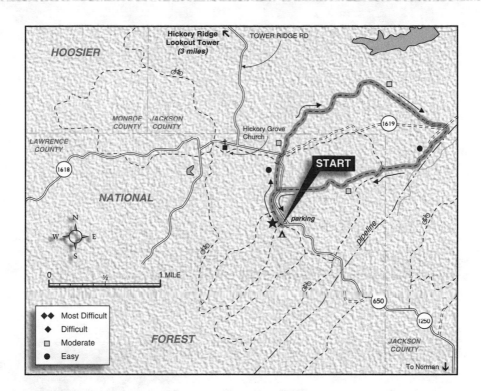

MILES   DIRECTIONS

0.0   **START** from the trailhead at the **northwest corner** of the **parking/ camping area**. Don't be fooled by the large "Hickory Ridge" information sign. That is not the trailhead.

0.3   Arrive at a **trail intersection**. Turn **left**.

0.4   Arrive at a **trail intersection**. Continue **straight**.

0.6   Cross a gravel road, continuing **straight** on the TRAIL.

0.8   Arrive at a **trail intersection**. Take the **left** split.

1.0   Bear **right** at the trail split. Traveling left will lead you into Hickory Ridge's northwestern loops.

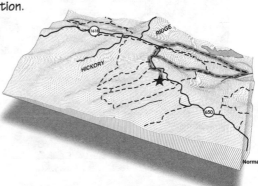

1.2   Arrive at a dirt road. Continue **straight** on the TRAIL, heading into the northeastern loops of the Hickory Ridge trail system.

3.3   The TRAIL crosses a gravel road and continues just off to the right of the road. Continue **straight** on the TRAIL.

3.4   The TRAIL dumps out into an open area at a trail intersection. Turn **right**. You are now traveling along the **pipeline portion** of the route.

3.6   The TRAIL heads back into the woods.

3.7   The TRAIL curves back toward the pipeline, then into the woods again.

4.1   Arrive at a **trail intersection**. Turn **left**.

4.2   Cross the **creek** and arrive at a **trail intersection**. Turn **right**

View along the pipeline section of Hickory Ridge.

Ride Information

Trail Maintenance Hotline:
 Hoosier National Forest   (812) 275-5987
  811 Constitution Ave.
  Bedford, IN 47421
 Brownstown Ranger District   (812) 358-2675
  608 West Commerce St.
  Brownstown, IN 47220

Group Rides:
 Sundays at 12:00 p.m.   (812) 339-3457
  Bicycle Garage
  507 E. Kirkwood
  Bloomington, IN 47408

Maps:
 USGS maps: Norman, IN; Elkinsville, IN

---

following the **TRAIL** as it immediately bends left. Turning left at this intersection leads to the southwestern loop.

5.2 Arrive at a **gravel road**. Cross the road and continue **straight** on the **TRAIL**.

5.21 Arrive at a **trail intersection** soon after the gravel road. Turn **left**.

5.5 Arrive at a **trail intersection**. Continue **straight**.

5.7 Arrive at a **trail intersection**. Take the **left** split.

6.0 The ride finishes back at the **parking area/campground**. Are you ready for one of the other loops now?

21   Shirley Creek Mtn Bike Trails

Ride Specs

Start: Shirley Creek Campground

Length: 9.1 miles of 11-mile system

Rating: Moderate

Terrain: Hilly; wooded singletrack and forest roads

Riding Time: 2 hours

Other Activities: Hiking, horseback riding, camping

Two things are unique to the Shirley Creek trail system. The first is the Lost River. In this karst that surrounds the trail, sinkholes, caverns, and underground waterways are common. As one of the longest subterranean waterways, the Lost River flows underground southeast of Orleans and runs south of Orangeville, eventually flowing into the East Fork of the White River.

The second thing unique to Shirley Creek is NBA superstar Larry Bird. Deemed the "Hick from French Lick," Bird did not actually grow up in French Lick. Just down the road a piece from Shirley Creek is Bird's real hometown of West Baden. In fact, Bird's mom still resides in their hometown, and Larry sometimes stops by to mow his mother's grass.

But the resort areas in French Lick adopted Bird as their own hometown boy with high hopes of filling more rooms. Every resort town needs a hook, and what better hook could a Hoosier town have than a living basketball legend.

Away from the resorts is the campground for Shirley Creek Recreation Area. Like most Hoosier National Forest campgrounds, no fees or permits are

Getting There

☞ **From Bloomington** – Take **Hwy 37 south** approximately 25 miles to **Hwy 50**. Take **Hwy 50 west** 9.6 miles to the intersection of **Hwy 50** and **Hwy 60**. Continue **west** on **Hwy 50** 0.1 miles to the first county road on the left. Turn **left** on this **county road** and immediately cross some railroad tracks. Drive 0.9 to **County Road 825 west**. Turn **right** on **County Road 825 west**. Drive 3.4 miles to the split in the road. Take the **left split** (**County Road 810 north**) and pass **Bonds Chapel** and a cemetery on the right. Drive 1.3 miles to **County Road 775**. This intersection is marked by a small grocery store on the right. Turn **right** on **County Road 775** and drive 1.2 miles to the **"Shirley Creek Trailhead"** sign on the **left**. Turn **left** into the property and follow the road to the **campgrounds**.

needed for camping. The grounds include primitive sites, pit toilets, and hitching racks at each site to tie off your weary bicycles or to air out your musty sleeping bag. Unfortunately, there is no drinking water here.

Generally, there is little activity in the campground except for the few equestrians who come to enjoy the trails. This is a group, though, that is friendly and approachable. So take the opportunity to talk to the people with whom you share the trails. A friendly conversation and an invitation to share a campfire will go a lot further to enhance relationships than any legislative hearing ever will. Talk about the trail, show them the maps from this book, and pass on some of the trail's highlights or caution areas.

The idea behind this stretch of national forest is to escape civilization for a while, breath fresh air, and enjoy the untouched, undeveloped beauty of the forest. The only difference between you and equestrians is your choice of transportation.

A positive attitude will be helpful at the start of this ride. Shift into your granny gear to begin this predominantly singletrack system, as the trailhead is marked by a quick ascent that climbs to the ridgetop and away from the campground. After this climb, the path levels off and crosses County Road 775. The route then rolls under a thick forest canopy and past a small deer pond. Cyclists are now just south of Hindostan. Until the 1820s, with the Hindostan Whetstone Company as its keystone, the town was a thriving stone-cutting hub. But when an unknown disease swept through the area, Hindostan was transformed into a ghost town.

After passing the trail that leads to Hindostan, the path bends to the west. As the singletrack heads toward Bonds Chapel, it holds a series of challenging climbs and descents that finish at County Road 810. The loop follows the county roads and offers a nice scenic break before heading back into the woods.

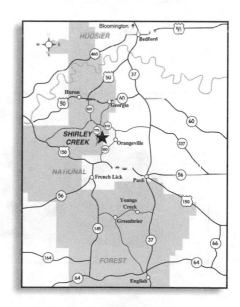

Just off the dirt road, the trail descends to a gate. A quick climb then takes cyclists back to the ridgetop. The system follows the contours and eventually drops back into Felknor Hollow at the southwestern corner and lowest point of the route. Here the path follows the creek bed for a short distance. During high-water season, cyclists will have to walk or ride along the creekbank.

The climb out of the lower landscape proves to be challenging as the trail ascends from 500 feet to the 800-foot ridge. After the climb, the route crosses back to County Road 775 and heads toward the campground.

MILES   DIRECTIONS

0.0   **START** at the **Shirley Creek Campground**. Find the **trailhead** at the **north end** of the **campground**.

0.1   The trail splits. Take the **right split**.

0.6   The trail splits. Take the **right split**.

0.7   The trail crosses **County Road 775**. Continue **straight** on **singletrack**.

0.8   The trail splits. Take the **right split**.

1.1   Arrive at a "T." Take the **left trail**.

1.5   The main trail bends to the **right**.

1.55   Pass a **deer pond** on the right.

1.6   The trail splits. Take the **left split**. The right split leads to **Hindostan**.

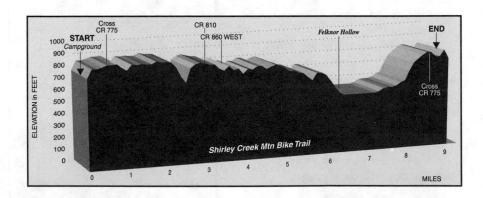

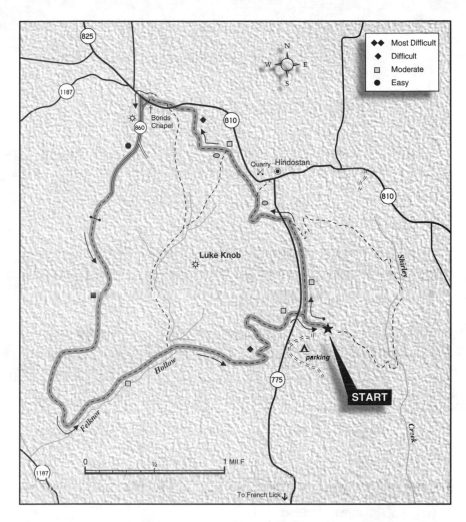

2.0 The trail splits. Take the **right split** and a pass **deer pond** on the left.

2.25 Come to a faint trail split to the right. Stay on the **MAIN TRAIL** to the **left**.

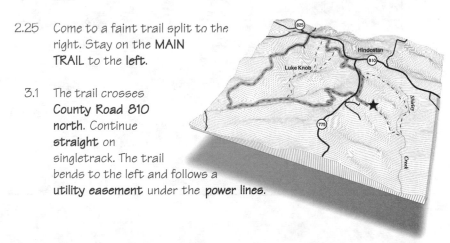

3.1 The trail crosses **County Road 810 north**. Continue **straight** on singletrack. The trail bends to the left and follows a **utility easement** under the **power lines**.

3.2   The trail bends back into the woods.

3.3   The trail intersects with **County Road 810 north**. Turn **right** onto COUNTY ROAD 810.

3.4   Turn **left** on COUNTY ROAD 860 WEST. Now riding on a **gravel road**.

4.0   **COUNTY ROAD 860 WEST** ends. Arrive at a trail split. Take the **left split**.

4.2   Come to an **open area**. Find the trail on the left. Roll past the **gate** and continue on the trail.

4.3   Pass a trail heading off to the left. Continue **straight** on the main trail.

4.8   The trail splits. Take the **left split**.

6.0   Come to an **open area**. Continue **straight** across the open area and find the trailhead.

6.3   A faint trail goes off to the left. Continue **straight** on the main trail.

6.35   Arrive at a **trail intersection** and a **trail marker**. Follow the trail and marker to the **left**. The trail takes a **hairpin turn** and actually

---

Ride Information

Trail Maintenance Hotline:

    Hoosier National Forest   (812) 275-5987
        811 Constitution Ave.
        Bedford, IN 47421

    Brownstown Ranger District   (812) 358-2675
        608 West Commerce St.
        Brownstown, IN 47220

Group Rides:

    Sundays at 12:00 p.m.   (812) 339-3457
        Bicycle Garage
        507 E. Kirkwood
        Bloomington, IN 47408

Maps:

    USGS maps: Huron, IN; Georgia, IN

follows the creekbed
through **Felknor Hollow**.

> ### Trail Adoption
>
> Cyclists can help maintain this trail by adopting a portion of it. For more information, call or write the *Brownstown Ranger Office*.
>
> (812) 358-2675

6.5 Through Felknor Hollow, the trail crosses a **singletrack intersection**. Continue **straight** along the creek bed.

6.55 A singletrack trail veers to the left of the creekbed at the bend. Take the **singletrack** to the **left**.

6.6 A trail merges in from the right. Continue **straight** on the main trail.

6.7 The trail crosses a **creekbed**. Continue **straight** on the trail.

7.0 The trail crosses a **creekbed**. Continue **straight** on the trail.

7.3 The trail intersects with a creekbed. Turn **left** along the **creek bed**, then a quick **right** back onto singletrack.

8.6 A trail goes off to the left. Continue **straight** on the MAIN TRAIL.

8.7 The trail crosses **County Road 775**. Continue **straight** on singletrack.

8.72 The trail comes to a "T" Take a **right**.

8.9 The trail empties out onto a **gravel road**. Turn **left** on the GRAVEL ROAD. Now heading back to the campground.

9.1 Reach **Shirley Creek Campground**.

22 Youngs Creek Trail

Ride Specs

Start: Trailhead parking area

Length: 10.8 miles

Rating: Difficult

Terrain: Hilly; wooded singletrack

Riding Time: 2½ hours

Other Activities: Hiking, horseback riding

Just east of the Youngs Creek Trailhead, near the town of Pine Valley, is a historical marker for the Indiana Initial Point Memorial. Established in 1805 by Ebenezer Buckingham, Jr., Initial Point marks the intersection of the Second Principal Meridian and the Baseline (the point of origin for all Indiana land surveys). The marker is also a tribute to all the frontiersmen who helped survey the state.

When the point of origin was surveyed, Pine Valley was known as Valley of Hog's Defeat. The origin of this name can be tied to a colorful tale claiming that several irate citizens drove off the feeding herds of hogs that once threatened to destroy their farmland. Over the years, the town thankfully changed its name to Pine Valley.

The Indiana Initial Point Memorial was dedicated to frontier surveyors in 1973, but the stone cutters who crafted the marker apparently left out the stanza that stands as a tribute to the cyclists who survived the Youngs Creek Trail ride.

Youngs Creek is one of the state's most difficult trail systems and is the most appealing for hard-core mountain bikers. The trail itself is a topographer's nightmare because of its constant need to descend, ascend, twist, and turn every 20 yards or so. The few flat spots on this loop are covered with muddy quagmires that provide resistance equal to a challenging climb. Even the county roads that make up a small portion of the trail harbor a substantial grade.

The trail begins from the north end of the parking area. In the first 1.5 miles, there are two climbs, both followed by sharp descents (one of which is a

---

Getting There

☞ **From Bloomington** – Travel **south** on **Hwy 37** approximately 60 miles to **Pine Valley**. At Pine Valley, turn **right** at the **Youngs Creek** sign, traveling **west** on **County Road 560 south**. Go 0.8 miles and turn **right** into the **trailhead parking area**. Only sign is a post marked "FR 707."

Pine-needle carpets offer a smooth ride for the cyclist.

white-knuckle switchback descent that leads down to a creekbed).

The rest areas of this system are not limestone ledges like the ones found on other trails in this area. The breaks on this loop come on the gravel roads that pop up at regular intervals along the route. The first rest stop occurs after the initial climbs and descents, but doesn't last long. It quickly leads back to more singletrack, and one short mile later, cyclists will drop down another switchback descent into a creekbed.

During this descent, cyclists will cross over an invisible Indian Treaty Line—one of many treaties that was made as settlers pushed Native Americans west.

Three miles into the ride the trail offers a cul-de-sac stopping place. It is actually a turnaround for campers, but offers a great rest area as well. One-half mile away from this rest stop, the trail intersects with a gravel road. There should be a sign here warning cyclists of a rooster crossing. This isn't a flock of *wild roosters*, though. Their home is up the road a bit.

Once the trail leads back into the woods, it turns into mud. This quagmire provides equal resistance to any of the day's toughest climbs, and a thick forest canopy overhead seems to keep it wet most of the year.

At the five-mile mark, the trail offers yet another thrilling technical descent. This downhill is fairly straight, and cyclists can carry some speed all the way to the creekbed. One mile later, the trail intersects with County Road

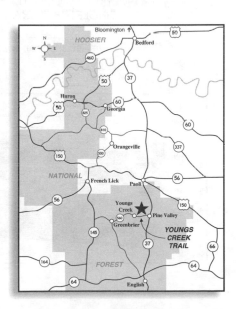

560, which leads cyclists back to the parking area.

This is a nice bailout point if supplies are low or if cyclists believe that bonking is eminent. If you choose to continue, this paved road offers only a short break. Once the turn is made on County Road 175, a smaller gear is recommended to make this climb to the trailhead—and the grade doesn't stop here, either.

Finally, after one mile of climbing, the grade tops out and the trail continues along the ridgetop. After a couple more miles of singletrack, cyclists climb a lengthy hill that tops out at County Road 560 and the parking area.

After the ride, cyclists can find a good spot to pitch a tent or sling a hammock at Youngs Creek campground. Like many of the Hoosier National Forest recreation areas, camping is free and open to anyone. The campground is located north of the trailhead parking area at the northernmost point of the trail. There are primitive sites available, the only amenities being pit toilets, hitching racks, and a picnic shelter.

MILES   DIRECTIONS

0.0   **START** at the north end of the **trailhead parking area**.

0.5   Bear **left** at the trail split, following the trail signs.

1.3   Bear **right** at the faint trail split. Ride down a number of switchbacks to Youngs Creek.

1.5   Cross **Youngs Creek**. Continue **straight**.

1.6   Turn **left** on the **GRAVEL ROAD**. Immediately turn **right** back onto the **SINGLETRACK TRAIL**.

2.0   Turn **right** at the trail split.

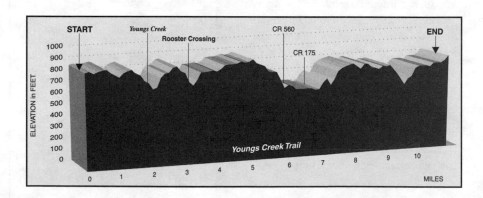

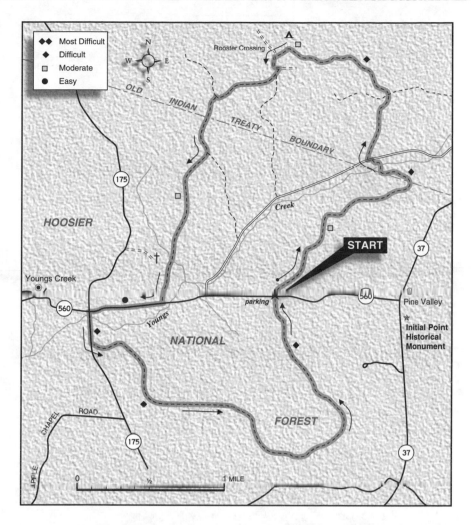

3.1 Arrive at a turnaround for campers. Ride **straight,** crossing this "cul-de-sac," and look for the **MAIN TRAIL** sign.

3.5 Turn **left** on the **GRAVEL ROAD.** Watch out for roosters crossing your path!

3.6 Continue **straight.** Pass a gravel road heading off to the right. This is private property and home of the roosters.

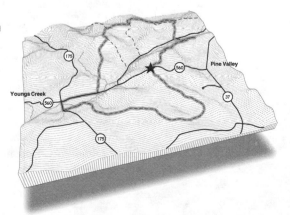

Ride Information

Trail Maintenance Hotline:

Hoosier National Forest   (812) 275-5987
    811 Constitution Ave.
    Bedford, IN 47421

Tell City Ranger District   (812) 547-7051
    248 15th Street
    Tell City, IN 47586

Maps:

USGS map: Valeene, IN

3.62   Follow the **singletrack gravel split** to the **right**.

3.65   Take the **right split** off the gravel trail.

3.7   Arrive at a **trail intersection**. Turn **right** on a DOUBLETRACK TRAIL.

4.9   Bear **left** at the trail split.

5.2   Continue on the main trail, following the signs to the right.

5.5   Cross a creekbed after a technical descent.

5.9   Turn **right** on COUNTY ROAD 560 SOUTH. You can turn left and head back to the parking area from here if you're tired.

6.4   Turn **left** on COUNTY ROAD 175 WEST. Don't be deceived by the pavement. CR 175 West has a climb worthy of respect.

6.6   Keep your eyes peeled for the trailhead marker on the left. Turn **left** onto a SINGLETRACK TRAIL.

7.3   Reach the summit of the most difficult climb in this loop.

7.6   The trail splits. Take the MAIN TRAIL to the **right**.

8.1   Take the trail to the **right**, following the trail sign.

8.4   Follow the trail sign to the **left**.

10.8   Reach **County Road 560 South**. Turn **right**, then a quick **left** into the **trailhead parking area**. Back at last!

23 Birdseye Trail

Ride Specs

Start: Parking area beside dirt road

Length: 6 miles of 10-mile system

Rating: Easy to Moderate

Terrain: Easy-grade forest roads

Riding Time: 1 – 1½ hours

Other Activities: Hiking, horseback
       riding, fishing

Not to be confused with the successful frozen vegetable brand, the Birdseye Trail is sandwiched between Ferdinand State Forest to the south and the town of Birdseye to the north.

It seems Birdseye was named after local clergyman, state legislator, and postmaster Reverend Benjamin Talbott Goodman, whose nickname was "Bird." In 1856, the residents of the area's main crossroads desired a post office. After surveying the proposed location, Goodman supposedly proclaimed, "It suits Bird's eye to a T-y-tee," which is about as believable as any Hoosier tale I've heard.

With a booming lumber industry, as well as a 1903 newspaper headline proclaiming, "Birdseye May Become Oil Center of The U.S.," the town became a bustling center. Drillers rushed in, leased the land, and constructed their wells. This early petroleum production was very intense and conservation policies were nonexistent. By and by, the wells dried up, the boom was over, and Birdseye bustled no more. Today, near that same intersection where Goodman took in his bird's-eye view, lies an antique shop, a city park, a few abandoned brick buildings, and Birdseye's historic post office.

Through all of the town's ups and downs, Birdseye plays host to yet another Hoosier National Forest off-the-beaten-path trail system. With a parking area that's nothing more than a notch off the county road, cyclists should see few other trail users during their ride.

This loop consists predominantly of wide paths and a few climbs blessed

---

Getting There

☞ **From Evansville** – Go **north** on I-164 approximately 12 miles to I-64. Take **I-64 east** 43 miles to Hwy 145 (**Exit 72**). Take **Hwy 145 north** for 6 miles to the **Birdseye Loop** sign. Turn **right** at this sign, heading **east** on the dirt road. Turn **right** into the **parking area** after 1½ miles. The parking area is little more than a widened fire road with a gate marking the trailhead.

This less-demanding ride affords more time to be spent looking for wildlife. Moo!

with forgiving grades. This combination makes the ride enjoyable and some-what suitable for introducing a novice to a backwoods bicycle ride.

A word of caution: motorized travel along this trail is prohibited, though locals use this area to go mudding with ATVs, motorcycles, and, judging by the large paths, four-wheel-drive trucks. Yielding to all motorized vehicles is highly recommended.

Away from the drone of revving engines, a rhythmic knocking can be heard from a distant tree. The source is a head-banging raptor known as a pileated woodpecker. These birds are common in southern Indiana and are easy to spot. With a carrot-top head and black body, these large birds can be seen scampering up and down trees tapping out their nests or looking for food.

Since this ride is less demanding than others, more time can be spent looking for wildlife such as deer, raccoons, turkey vultures, and red-tailed hawks. The beginning of the route travels along a fire road that leads to the system's only lake. The trail follows the edge of the lake for a short while as it winds along a wooded bank.

Once out of the trees, cyclists will find the first climb. This is also one of the

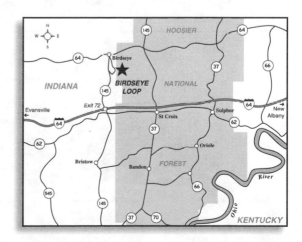

high-traffic areas for four wheelers. From this point, all the way to the Anderson River, the trail travels along a flat fire road. As soon as you cross the river, you'll come upon the first and only section of singletrack.

This is the most challenging section of the loop, which includes the ride's only difficult climb. This section provides a nice change of pace, leading out to the dirt road that will take you back to your vehicle.

As far as camping is concerned, overnight accommodations can be found at Ferdinand State Forest. The state park literature claims that Ferdinand has some of the prettiest campsites in the state. There are 68 campsites with seven primitive sites circling the 42-acre lake. Swimming, fishing, and boating are the main attractions here. All in all, Birdseye will suit mountain bikers to a "T-y-tee!"

MILES   DIRECTIONS

0.0   **START** from the **parking area** beside the dirt road. Head **south** from the parking area to the **BIRDSEYE TRAIL.**

0.2   The trail bends to the **left** into the woods.

0.4   The trail empties into an open field. The trail here is faint. Follow the **right perimeter** of the field.

0.5   The trail crosses over the small lake's dam. In late summer, waves of grasshoppers dive for cover from your wheels as you pass.

0.51   The trail bends to the right and heads back into the woods.

1.5   Begin the first climb on the trail.

1.7   The trail splits. Take the **right split**.

2.2   Cross a small creek.

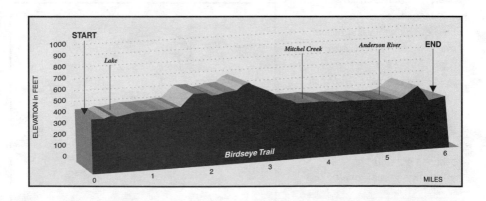

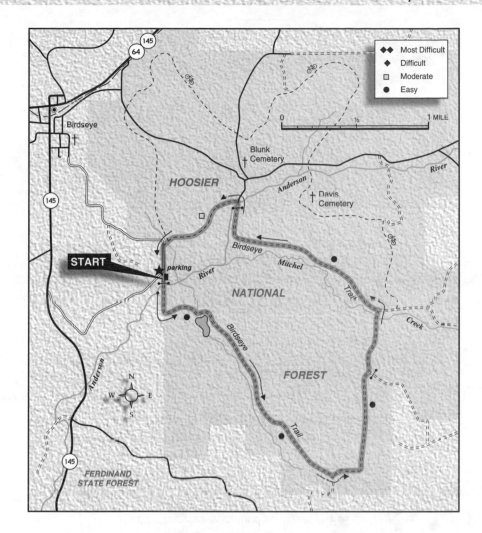

2.4   Arrive at a **trail intersection**. Take the **left trail**. Cross a creek.

2.5   Begin the second notable climb of the trail.

3.0   Arrive at a **trail intersection**. Continue **straight**.

3.2   Pass a gate and a trail on the right. Continue straight.

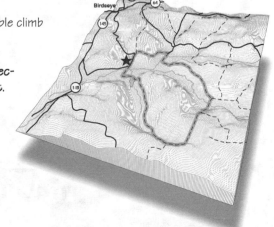

Ride Information

Trail Maintenance Hotline:

Hoosier National Forest   (812) 275-5987
    811 Constitution Ave.
    Bedford, IN 47421
Tell City Ranger District   (812) 547-7051
    248 15th Street
    Tell City, IN 47586

Maps:

USGS map: Birdseye, IN

3.7   Cross **Mitchel Creek**. Turn **left** on a **DIRT ROAD**. Following the dirt road to the right will take you to the longer loop to the north.

5.2   Cross a bridge over the **Anderson River**. Turn **left** off the dirt road onto a **SINGLETRACK TRAIL**.

5.3   Begin the third notable climb of the trail.

5.4   Reach the summit of the climb, cross an open field, and then head back into the woods.

5.6   **BIRDSEYE TRAIL** dumps out into an open field and bends to the right. The trail then follows the **right perimeter** of the field.

5.9   The singletrack intersects with a gravel road. Turn **left** on the **GRAVEL ROAD**.

6.1   Return to the **trailhead parking area**. Ride complete.

Oriole Trail 24

Ride Specs

Start: Jeffries Cemetery

Length: 6.3 miles of 10-mile system

Rating: Easy to Moderate

Terrain: Easy-grade forest roads

Riding Time: 1 – 1½ hours

Other Activities: Hiking, horseback riding

You can get your kicks on Indiana's Route 66. The singer wasn't talking about the anonymous Hoosier route; nonetheless, that didn't stop many turn-of-the-century folks from getting *their* kicks out here!

During the Civil War, would-be oil drillers struck mineral water instead of black crude near the town of Sulphur Springs. Instead of being set back, the drillers made lemonade from lemons. They switched hats, became developers, and opened the White Sulphur Resort, bottling and selling their newly discovered powerful placebo. Vacationers and clients consumed the ill-tasting waters, but boasted of its medicinal powers; they kept the three-story resort in business for many years.

Records don't show when the hotel went belly-up, but it's possible that at least one of the founders is buried in Jeffries Cemetery. Since you are parking at the foot of many, if not all, of the Jeffries who made this area their home, it is customary to climb the steps of the cemetery and pay your respects to the family. The plot of R.B. Jeffries, who died in 1872, looks to be the oldest stone.

With homage out of the way, pull your bike off the rack and begin the ride. With the small parking lot and lack of trailhead signs, solitary cyclists can enjoy this somewhat anonymous trail.

Riding this quiet trail will bring you close to many white-tailed deer. Although it may be hard to believe, white-tailed deer were once eliminated from Indiana. They were reintroduced in the 1940s, and

Getting There

☞ **From Evansville** – Go **north** on I-164 approximately 12 miles to I-64. Take **I-64 east** 57 miles to **Hwy 37/Hwy 66 west (Exit 86)**. Go **south** on **Hwy 66 west** 4½ miles to **Jeffries Cemetery**. Look for a small **Hoosier National Forest** sign on the **left** side of the road. Turn **left** into the **parking area**.

with careful management they now flourish and can be found in every county in the state.

Hunting is permitted here, as in many other Hoosier National Forest recreation areas. Hunters will often set up deer camps in the parking areas. With hunters dressed in camouflaged gear and cyclists clad in Lycra, the gap between the groups can seem fairly wide. (See sidebar on page 179.)

Oriole Trail is made up predominantly of forest roads and features an occasional climb. Most descents are on a fairly easy grade, with the most memorable ones along the gravel road. The beginning of the trail is adequately maintained, but at the first turn, cyclists will find themselves riding through knee-high grass. Following the tire tracks on the road is like riding parallel singletrack.

During the late summer months, spiders like to spin their webs across this somewhat abandoned section of trail. Rolling along on an early morning ride, with cobwebs covering your face, will either cause uncontrollable convulsions or banishment of your arachnophobia!

Two miles into the ride and out of the webs, the fire road intersects with a gravel road. Here lies your fastest descent of the day. Be careful, though, to ride this one at your own pace. The loose gravel is challenging and can be a bit intimidating. After the downhill, the trail follows the gravel road for the next 1.5 miles before turning back onto a fire road.

The fire road winds north and northwest, climbs slightly near the gate, and returns to Jeffries Cemetery.

The downside of this unkept, rugged trail, especially in the sections where you are pedaling through the knee-high grass, is that it is prime ground for ticks. A brochure, distributed at the Hoosier National Forest offices, recommends precautions while riding in tick-infested areas. (See sidebar on page 178.)

Checking for ticks after a ride through the woods or the weeds is as essen-

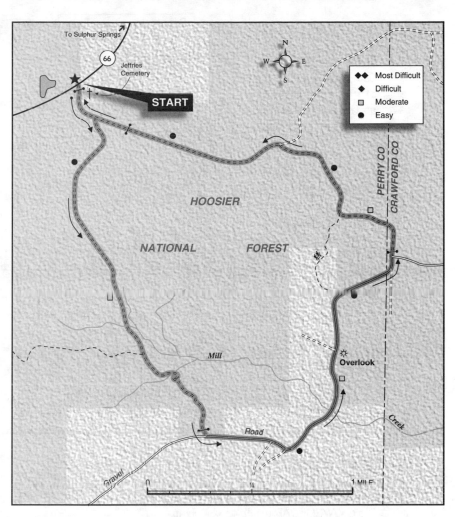

tial as replacing fluids. One bout with Lyme disease will provide a lasting reminder for this. An ounce of prevention and one coat of tick-repellent spray is helpful to stop the bloodsuckers from latching on to any bare skin.

Early signs of Lyme disease include a slowly expanding rash and flu-like symptoms. Left untreated, Lyme disease can cause a form of arthritis resulting in aching joints, swelling, dizziness, an irregular heartbeat, or a weakening of facial muscles.

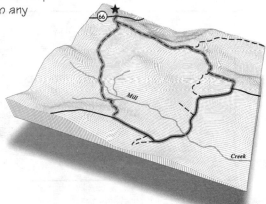

MILES   DIRECTIONS

0.0   **START** at **Jeffries Cemetery**. The trail starts from the gate at the **southwest corner** of the **parking area**.

0.2   The trail splits. Take the **right** split.

1.7   Cross **Mill Creek**. The trail does a 180-degree turn then switches back.

1.71   The trail does another 180-degree turn and begins to ascend.

2.4   Roll past a gate and turn **left** on the **GRAVEL ROAD**. Now on a fast descent. Beware of the loose gravel.

3.1   Cross **Mill Creek**. The road bends slightly left and begins to ascend.

3.7   The **GRAVEL ROAD** bends to the right.

4.0   The **GRAVEL ROAD** bends to the left. There is a logging road to

---

Protection From Ticks

- Avoid tick habitats. (We as mountain bikers know this to be impossible, so we will ignore this tip.)
- Dress properly if you must go into a tick habitat. (Shaved legs covered to mid-thigh with Lycra shorts are not the best tick-repelling clothes.)
- Check for and remove any ticks on you or others in your company as soon as possible after leaving a tick habitat. (This is the best preventive tip for mountain bikers. But beware that this can resemble a primate social activity. To avoid any resemblance to primates, refrain from eating the ticks that you pull from your group members.)
- Check pets for ticks and use tick-control pet products. (Hot match heads are still one of the best removal methods. Alcohol also works.)

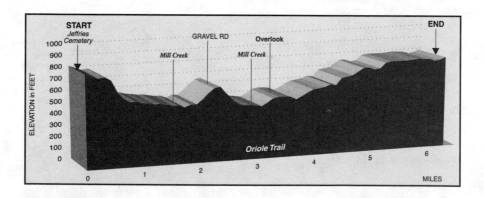

Hunters vs Mountain Bikers

During deer hunting season (Bow season: November 16-December 1; Shotgun season: October 1-15 and December 7-31), especially during opening weekends when hunters are feeling the most zealous, it's best to follow these precautions:

- Wear an orange hat or orange vest. If you can't stretch a hat over your helmet, opt for the hat.
- Avoid riding early in the morning. Allow hunters to have their prime time. Ride late in the morning and early in the afternoon.
- Make noise when you ride. Don't shuffle quietly behind the bushes. You don't want to be mistaken for game. Just ask Greg LeMond about this one. He still has the shotgun pellets lodged in his body.

the right, but stay on the gravel road to the left.

4.1 Turn left on the **LOGGING ROAD** past the gate.

4.5 Arrive at a faint trail split. Take the **left split**.

4.55 The trail splits. Take the **right split**.

5.1 The trail splits. Take the **left split**.

6.0 Pass through an open gate.

6.3 Return to the **parking area** and **Jeffries Cemetery**.

Ride Information

Trail Maintenance Hotline:
Hoosier National Forest   (812) 275-5987
    811 Constitution Ave.
    Bedford, IN 47421
Tell City Ranger District   (812) 547-7051
    248 W. 15th Street
    Tell City, IN 47586

Maps:
    USGS map: Beechwood, IN

25 Tipsaw Lake

Ride Specs

Start: Swimming/picnic area parking lot

Length: 6 miles

Rating: Easy with moderate climbs

Terrain: Flat; wooded singletrack

Riding Time: 1 hour

Other Activities: Hiking, camping, fishing, swimming

Tipsaw Lake is the newest recreation area in Hoosier National Forest. The lake draws its water from Sulphur Fork Creek, Massey Branch, Snake Branch, and other smaller tributaries, and is surrounded by one of the best introductory mountain bike trail systems in the national forest. This six-mile loop gives novices a taste of rugged singletrack, as well as some moderate climbs. At the end of the ride, cyclists can reward themselves with a cool dip in the lake.

Tipsaw Lake is in view during most of the ride, and the finish of this ride can be seen from across the 130-acre lake, offering tired riders hope that they can continue to the finish.

The trail begins as a paved path that leads away from the picnic area. It changes to gravel and cuts across the boat-launch parking lot before leading to the first section of singletrack. The first part of the trail switches between woods and grassy fields before circling around the east end of the lake.

Once around this section of the lake, the trail cuts through a couple of open fields before returning to the wooded singletrack. From this point, the lake stays in view for the majority of the ride.

As the trail merges with a dirt road, you will come across the first of three spots that look as if they were designed specifically to offer a respite to leg-weary cyclists and hikers. At the three-mile mark, come to a dirt-road turnaround and what resembles a mini limestone Stonehenge. This group of stone benches offers a place to stretch out or lean your bike as you skip rocks across the lake.

Getting There

☞ **From Evansville** – Take **I-164 north** approximately 12 miles to I-64. Take **I-64 east** 51 miles to **Hwy 37 south** (**Exit 80**). Take **Hwy 37 south** approximately 6½ miles to **Tipsaw Lake Recreation Area**. Turn **right** on the **Park Entrance Road** and drive 3 miles to the **swimming/picnic area parking lot**.

Please tread lightly for their sake.

For cemetery buffs interested in seeing Lanman Cemetery, the second stop comes just after the first. Down the road a short distance past Stonehenge, there is a small path off to the left that leads to the cemetery.

The third rest area affords the best view along this ride. This break comes four miles into the ride as the trail rolls over the dam. During the summer, knee-high grass sways in the breeze and the full view of the lake and surrounding wooded hills is quite dramatic. Take time for a little lizard spotting; blue-tailed skinks and other small lizards like to run through the grass here.

After rolling across the open area near the dam, prepare to ride the more challenging portion of the trail. The singletrack twists around the lake and leads to a few challenging climbs. For beginners, just remember the final leg of the trail and the beach are near.

After the ride, activities at the swimming beach will easily fill the remainder of the day. There is a boat ramp that permits electric motors, and panfishing here is rated as excellent. The beach is clean for swimming, but there is no lifeguard on duty.

As far as camping is considered, Tipsaw offers 44 sites to weary travelers. The amenities include water, flush toilets, showers, and electricity on roughly half the sites. Primrose and Goldenrod

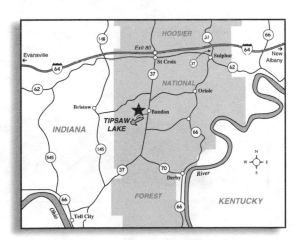

are group campsites that can be rented for $25 per night. The five-star campsite is in the Catbriar Loop, and it can be rented for $45 per night. It has electrical hookups, lights, and a shelter.

Fifteen picnic sites, two shelters, a modern changing area, and horseshoe pits line the north shore of the lake. If you lose track of time on a sunny day, look to the sundial near the bathhouse to see how late you really are.

MILES　DIRECTIONS

0.0　**START** at the **swimming/picnic area parking lot.** Follow the **PAVED PATH** from the east end of the parking lot toward the boat ramp parking area. Roll past a shelter as the path turns to gravel.

0.1　**GRAVEL PATH** crosses into the **boat ramp parking area.** Continue **straight.**

0.15　Turn **left** out of the parking lot, then a quick **right** at the trailhead following the singletrack **HIKE/BIKE TRAIL** east.

0.2　Arrive at a **trail intersection.** Continue **straight.**

0.6　Cross a creek. Continue **straight.**

1.0　Arrive at a **trail intersection.** Bear **right** around the gate.

1.1　Bear **hard right.** Now at the east end of the loop.

1.25　**HIKE/BIKE TRAIL** crosses an open field, traveling **straight** along the right perimeter of the field.

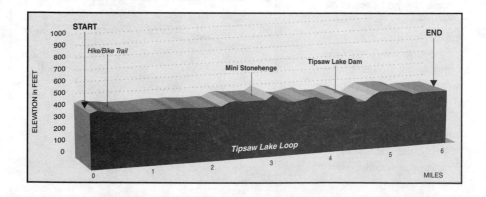

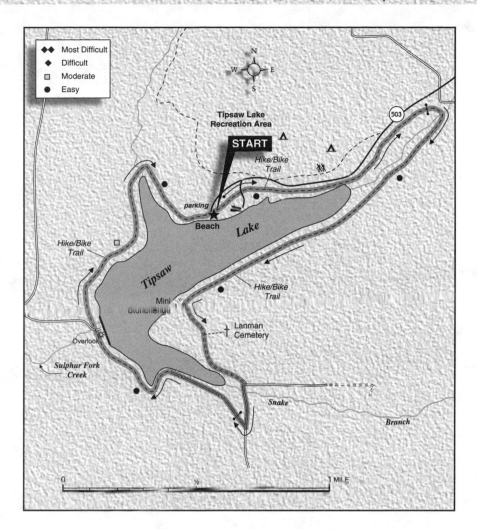

Legend
◆◆ Most Difficult
◆ Difficult
☐ Moderate
● Easy

Tipsaw Lake
Recreation Area

START

Hike/Bike
Trail

parking

Beach

Lake

Tipsaw

Hike/Bike
Trail

Hike/Bike
Trail

Mini
Stonehenge

Lanman
Cemetery

Overlook

Sulphur Fork
Creek

Snake

Branch

503

0   ½   1 MILE

2.2   The lake comes back into view.

3.1   Pass the **mini Stonehenge** on a
forest road turnaround. The
rocks on the edge of the lake
are a great place for a
break.

Tipsaw Lake
Recreation Area

Tipsaw   Lake

503

3.11   Arrive at a dirt road.
Turn **right** on the
DIRT ROAD.

3.3   Arrive at an **intersection**.
Turn **right** on the DIRT ROAD.

3.5   Come to a trailhead. Follow the signs and take the **HIKE/BIKE TRAIL** to the **right**. Pass a gate and cross a bridge. Now traveling on a **grass-covered fire road**.

3.8   Tipsaw Lake comes back into view.

4.0   Cross a creek and look for a trail marker to the right.

4.3   Come to a short, steep rise up to **Tipsaw Lake dam**. Wonderful view of Tipsaw Lake. **Lizards** are found here during the summertime.

4.8   The open grassy **HIKE/BIKE TRAIL** narrows to a singletrack and leads back into the woods.

5.2   Come to the first moderate climb.

5.5   **HIKE/BIKE TRAIL** splits. Take the right split.

5.9   The ride ends at the sidewalk that leads into the lake. Options include returning to your vehicle or taking a cool dip in the lake!

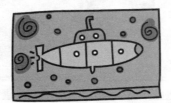

Ride Information

Trail Maintenance Hotline:
Hoosier National Forest   (812) 275-5987
    811 Constitution Ave.
    Bedford, IN 47421
Tell City Ranger District   (812) 547-7051
    248 W. 15th Street
    Tell City, IN 47586

Maps:
USGS maps: Bristow, IN; Gatchel, IN
Tipsaw Lake Recreation Area map and guide

26 Mogan Ridge Mtn Bike Trails

Ride Specs

Start: Radio tower parking area

Length: 6.6 miles of 11-mile system

Rating: Moderate

Terrain: Easy-grade forest roads and singletrack

Riding Time: 1 hour

Other Activities: Hiking, horseback riding

As you drive along the road that leads to Mogan Ridge, you might be greeted by an American kestrel. Commonly called sparrow hawks for their sparrow size and hawk features, kestrels can be spotted hovering at the road's edge above the high grass.

With greetings and salutations out of the way, it's time to take a look at the map. One can't help but notice that a portion of the Mogan Ridge route is shaped like South America. In tribute to jungles and rugged lands of our continental neighbor, the land of Mogan Ridge is also rugged and unkept. The benefit of such a route is less usage and a very quiet ride.

The majority of this trail is doubletrack, forest, and gravel roads. There is some singletrack on the backside of the trail, but it acts more as a connector between two forest road sections. Even though you are riding on forest roads, the lack of maintenance keeps even the wider areas fairly rugged.

The wild nature of this path can be traced to the fact that the trail was just recently opened for recreational use. In years past, this land was managed solely for timber, wild turkey, and other wildlife. Many of the trail markers are faded, but forest rangers are in the process of updating them.

Here, like many other places in the national forest, ginseng grows wild and can be harvested from August 15 to December 31. Hoosier National Forest officials have established guidelines for harvesting of this five-leaf plant. (Please see the "Harvesting Ginseng" sidebar on page 188.)

Getting There

☞ **From Evansville** – Go **north** on I-164 approximately 12 miles to I-64. Travel **east** on I-64 51 miles to Hwy 37 **south** (Exit 80). Go **south** on Hwy 37 approximately 18 miles to Hwy 70. Go **east** on Hwy 70 no more than 0.1 miles to Old Hwy 37. Travel **north** on Old Hwy 37 1.1 miles to the **Mogan Ridge** sign on the right side of the road. Turn **right**, traveling **east** on an unmarked gravel road for 0.4 miles to the **Radio Tower Parking Area** on the **left**. Look for the radio tower.

Many cultures believe ginseng is a general cure-all, as well as an aphrodisiac. So certain are some of ginseng's qualities that Asians have harvested their domestic crop almost to extinction. In America, many nutritional supplements use ginseng, and, as many veteran cyclists may already be aware, they have probably, at one time or another, consumed this popular herb. Other interesting facts and additional guidelines can be requested from any Hoosier National Forest office.

For the most part, the first part of the loop is easy going, without any notable climbs or descents. During the summer, the grass here is uncut and tickles your

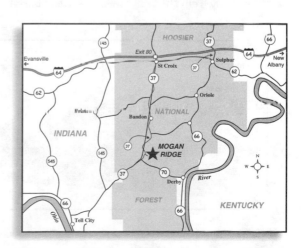

Harvesting Ginseng

- Observe the ginseng season.
- Collect ginseng after the berries have ripened.
- Plant the berries as you harvest the plant.
- Harvest only three or four prong plants. Leave the younger plants behind.

knees. As you approach the western portion of the loop, stay alert as there is a section that is not well marked, and getting lost is never much fun.

At 1.2 miles you'll come to an open field where the trail fades away. Using the fenceline on the right, follow it to the left until you come to an opening at a tree marked with a blue diamond sign.

After this marker, the path becomes a grass-covered doubletrack trail. This route slowly descends to the southernmost part of the loop, and the closest point you will be to civilization.

As you round Cape Horn (the southernmost section of the loop), you will see Highway 70. Remember this point if you have a flat and need a ride back to your car. Once around the horn, you will be approaching the loop's most challenging section. The first part, a forest road, follows the eastern portion of this loop (what could be considered the east coast of South America). The road climbs slightly, taking you from Argentina all the way to the coast of Brazil (get out your atlases folks), where the loop's most challenging section awaits.

Here you will find climbs that warrant this ride's moderate classification. There are a couple of tricky, sparsely marked sections here, but follow the directions and look for the faint blue diamonds on the tree trunks. These markers will help confirm that you are heading in the right direction.

As you circle around the northern section of the loop, the blue trail passes two trails that lead to the five-mile eastern section of this trail system. Here the trail also dumps out to a gravel road. This road harbors a swift descent then up another climb. After the rise, the road finally returns back to where you left your vehicle.

Away from the trail to the east, two burial grounds exist. Talley and

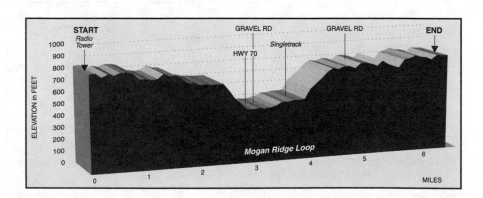

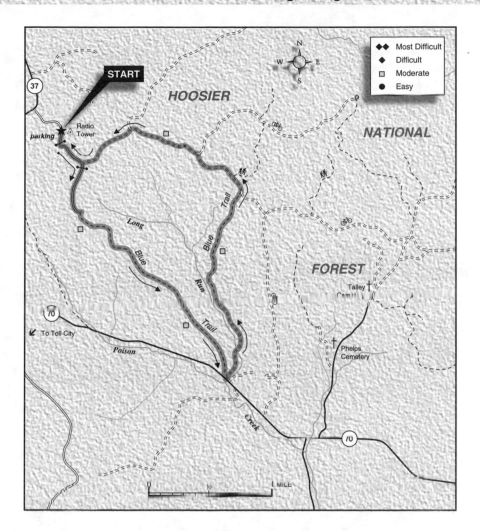

Map legend:
- ◆◆ Most Difficult
- ◆ Difficult
- □ Moderate
- ● Easy

START

37 parking Radio Tower

HOOSIER

NATIONAL

FOREST

Long Blue Blue Run Trail Trail

Talley Cemetery

70 To Tell City

Poison

Phelps Cemetery

Creek

70

N
W E
S

0   ½   1 MILE

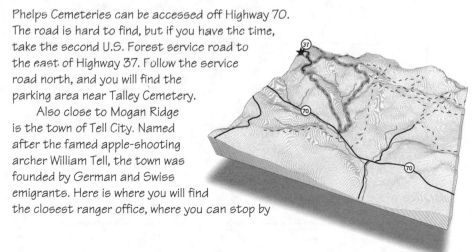

Phelps Cemeteries can be accessed off Highway 70.
The road is hard to find, but if you have the time,
take the second U.S. Forest service road to
the east of Highway 37. Follow the service
road north, and you will find the
parking area near Talley Cemetery.

Also close to Mogan Ridge
is the town of Tell City. Named
after the famed apple-shooting
archer William Tell, the town was
founded by German and Swiss
emigrants. Here is where you will find
the closest ranger office, where you can stop by

and purchase some maps or pick up some of their free literature.

Also in town is the Tell City Pretzel Company. Following Casper Goor's original recipe (one of the town's founders), these pretzels are hand-twisted, glazed, salted, baked, and made available to the public for a great post-ride snack that's also low in fat!

MILES   DIRECTIONS

0.0   START from the **Radio Tower Parking Area**. Turn **left** out of the parking area to the GRAVEL ROAD.

0.1   Roll past a gate.

0.2   Pass a faint trail on the right that merges into the main gravel trail. Continue **straight** on the GRAVEL ROAD.

0.3   Arrive at a **trail intersection**. Turn **right** and roll past a gate.

0.8   Trail becomes faint. Follow the **blue signs**, taking the **right split**.

1.2   Trail splits. Take the **center split**. Basically, just continue straight across the field and look for the **blue trail markers** on the fencepost until getting back into the woods.

1.6   Turn **left** into an open field. Roll through the grassy trail and find **blue trail marker** on a tree to the right.

1.7   Follow the **blue arrows** to the **left**.

2.7   Hwy 70 is now in view. Take the **FOREST ROAD** to the **left**.

3.8   Trail changes to singletrack.

Ride Information

Trail Maintenance Hotline:

Hoosier National Forest   (812) 275-5987
    811 Constitution Ave.
    Bedford, IN 47421

Tell City Ranger District   (812) 547-7051
    248 W. 15th Street
    Tell City, IN 47586

Maps:

USGS map: Derby, IN

4.4   Trail is not well marked here. Bear **left** at the split. There is a blue
      marker on the right just up the trail.

4.9   Trail dumps out onto a **GRAVEL ROAD**. Head west.

5.2   Arrive at a **trail intersection**. Stay **left** on the **GRAVEL ROAD**.
      Taking the road to the right leads to the eastern loops of Mogan
      Ridge.

5.9   Pass a logging road on the right. Stay on the **GRAVEL ROAD**. Now
      climbing one of the tougher climbs of the trail.

6.3   Pass the gate that marked the beginning of the loop. Continue
      straight on the GRAVEL ROAD.

6.6   Complete the loop and arrive back at the parking area. Time to
      grab some pretzels in Tell City!

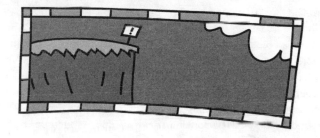

27 German Ridge Recreation Area

Ride Specs

Start: Day use parking lot

Length: 8.8 miles of 23-mile system

Rating: Moderate

Terrain: Wooded singletrack and forest roads

Riding Time: 45 minutes – 3 hours

Other Activities: Hiking, horseback riding, camping, swimming

German Ridge has the distinction of being the first recreation area in Hoosier National Forest. By using the sizable work force of the Civilian Conservation Corps, the U.S. Forest Service was able to develop the property during the years 1939-1940. On May 17, 1942, German Ridge was dedicated and became a role model for the establishment of other recreation areas in the forest.

However, during Civil War times, long before the CCC developed this recreation area, an attempted coup occurred, aimed at taking over this land. In 1863, Confederate Captain Thomas Hines led his troops across the Ohio River to contact southern sympathizers and their Copperhead organizations. But Hoosiers were not fooled into believing that Hines was leading a Union troop seeking deserters. When his coup was called, Hines' troop was wiped out and he and a few others narrowly escaped back to Kentucky.

A historical marker documenting these events is found east of German Ridge along Highway 66. Hines may have been better off looking for a place to ride his mountain bike than trying to start war. He could have enjoyed one of Indiana's deep south trail systems and avoided this little skirmish altogether.

For cyclists, this southernmost recreation area can provide a full weekend

Getting There

☞ **From Evansville** – Go **north** on I-164 approximately 12 miles to I-64. Take I-64 **east** 57 miles to Hwy 37/Hwy 66 (Exit 86). Take **Hwy 37 south** 2 miles to **Hwy 66 west**. Take **Hwy 66 west** (actually, the highway is heading south at this point) **south** to **Rome**. Drive 18 miles on **Hwy 66** and cross Hwy 70. Stay on **Hwy 66**. Follow signs to **German Ridge Recreation Area**. Travel 11.6 miles and turn **right** on **German Ridge Road**. Drive 0.8 miles and turn **left** at the **Hoosier National Forest** sign on the **Park Entrance Road**. Bear **left** into the **campground area**. At 0.5 miles turn **right** into the **Day Use Parking Area**.

Taking in some of the local scenery.

of riding. German Ridge spans 250 acres and holds 23 miles of trails. For cyclists looking to combine a weekend of trail riding and primitive camping, German Ridge is ideal.

The four-acre lake also offers other activities such as swimming and fishing. Additionally, there are some incredible hiking trails that are off limits to mountain bikes with many outcrops of sandstone worth checking out.

Unlike most Hoosier National Forest recreation areas, there is a fee for camping at German Ridge: $4 per night, $6 per night with horses, and $10 per night with horses on a double site. There are 20 campsites, 10 doubles and 10 singles. The sites are equipped with vault toilets, hitching racks to tie off the bikes, two hand-pump wells to fill water bottles, and a bonfire pit to burn discarded energy bar wrappers (non toxic only, of course).

The soils along this loop are extremely soft. Rangers encourage equestrians and cyclists to make as little impact on the area as possible, and park literature asks that equestrians and cyclists ride single file and avoid skirting puddles and minor obstacles so no further damage is done to the area. Also, if there are

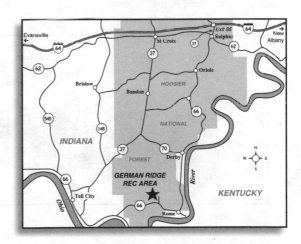

fallen logs or brush on the trail, take the time to remove them from the trail.

As you will see, there are some areas along the trail where these requests have been ignored. The result is a wide, swampy, and rutted track that is unrideable. Hopefully, over time the trail will be repaired and remain open.

Overall, the trails are a wonderful balance of singletrack and forest roads. There are some challenging climbs, but for the most part this area is very forgiving.

One possible stopping point of the ride is at the two-mile mark. At this deer pond, the grass and bank around the pond are a haven for various wildlife. Blue-tailed skinks can be found in the grass, while many birds use the pond to bathe and drink.

At the four-mile mark, another great resting spot awaits. A huge slab of limestone serves as a natural park bench and a place to take in some quiet time. There are also two old burial grounds to explore. The first comes at the 5½-mile mark. German Ridge Cemetery can be found just off Tower Road in the middle of the recreation area. The second is off the northern perimeter of the trail system. Schraner Cemetery sits at the northernmost point of the property and can be accessed via County Road 3.

MILES   DIRECTIONS

0.0   **START** from the **Day Use Parking Area** and follow the **MULTI-USE TRAIL** into the woods. This trail is marked with **horseshoes** to the right of the trail.

0.1   Cross the **Park Entrance Road**. Continue **straight** on the MULTI-USE TRAIL.

0.8   Arrive at a **trail intersection**. Bear **left** at the split. Going right returns you to the campground.

1.3   Cross a shallow creek. Pretty steady climb after the creek crossing.

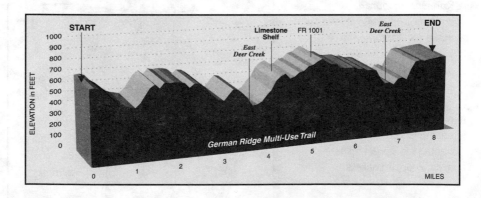

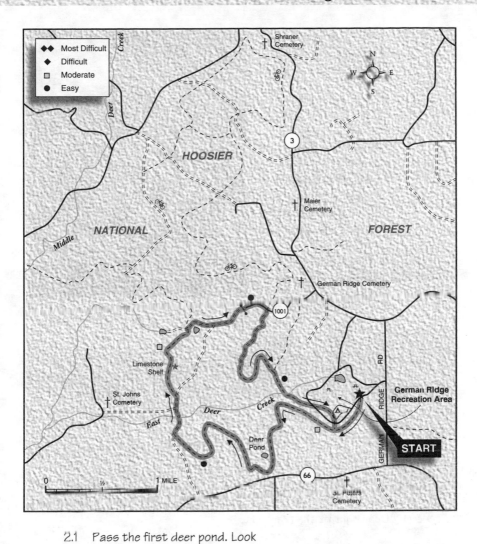

Most Difficult
Difficult
Moderate
Easy

HOOSIER

NATIONAL

FOREST

Middle

Shraner Cemetery

Maier Cemetery

German Ridge Cemetery

Deer

Creek

3

1001

Limestone Shelf

St. Johns Cemetery

East

Deer

Creek

German Ridge Recreation Area

RIDGE RD

GERMAN

START

Deer Pond

66

St. Peters Cemetery

0   ½   1 MILE

2.1 Pass the first deer pond. Look carefully and you might spot a blue-tailed skink.

3.9 Cross **East Deer Creek**.

4.2 Come to a descent rutted in deep horseshoe prints. This rutted trail doesn't help the equestrians' argument that horses do less damage to the trails than mountain bikes.

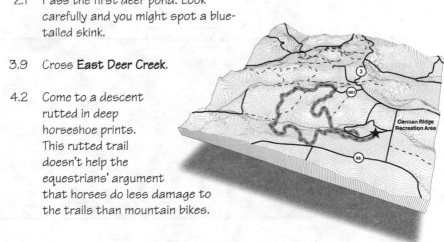

4.4 Arrive at a great **limestone shelf** and take a break.

4.8 Pass a deer pond.

5.1 Arrive at a **trail intersection**. Bear **right** following the **MAIN TRAIL** sign. The left trail leads to the northern loops of the German Ridge area.

5.7 Roll past a **gate** through a parking area. Continue **straight** on **LOGGING ROAD 1001**.

Multi-use trails make up most of the mountain bike trail systems in Hoosier National Forest.

5.8 **LOGGING ROAD 1001** splits. Take the **right** split.

6.0 Turn **right** at the trailhead sign on the right side of the road.

6.6 Pass a deer pond.

7.4 Cross a creek.

7.8 Cross **East Deer Creek**.

8.0 Bear **right** at the trail split.

Ride Information

Trail Maintenance Hotline:

Hoosier National Forest   (812) 275-5987
    811 Constitution Ave.
    Bedford, IN 47421

Tell City Ranger District   (812) 547-7051
    248 W. 15th Street
    Tell City, IN 47586

Maps:

    USGS map: Rome, IN

8.1 The trail crosses the **Park Entrance Road**. Turn **right** on the paved road.

8.4 **PARK ENTRANCE ROAD** crosses a trail. Continue **straight** on **PARK ENTRANCE ROAD**. The trail to the left leads to the campground.

8.6 Pass a gate that leads to the campground.

8.8 Turn **left** into the **Day Use Parking Lot** and finish up the ride.

28 Ogala Mtn Bike Trails

Ride Specs

Start: Parking off 1190 North Road

Length: 6.1 miles of 7-mile system

Rating: Easy to Moderate

Terrain: Wooded singletrack, dirt
         roads

Riding Time: 2 hours

Other Uses: Hiking, fishing

The Ogala Trail System is one that seems to thrive on the edge. Situated at the southern border of Brown County, and away from the hubbub of Nashville and Brown County State Park's tourist traps, Ogala resides peacefully in the quiet fringe of nature.

Ogala also seems to exist on the fringe of the Forest Service. Sitting like a diamond in the rough, this trail system is mostly undeveloped with many trails sparsely marked; fallen timber crossing some of its cut paths. Ogala's tranquil existence draws the solitary cyclist and will show off its gems only to the most peaceful trail users. Tucked back along these faint paths, wild turkey, grouse, many species of woodpecker, and deer all call the Ogala area home. On still winter afternoons, distant tapping of pileated and blackback woodpeckers are the forest's only sounds. While on the snow-covered ground, three-toed turkey tracks seem to saunter in all directions.

Originally, the Ogala property was accessed by forest roads. But these routes have not been maintained and today the wide paths have been reduced to singletrack. These one-lane routes make up the majority of the loop and cut through high grass where the dirt roads used to be. Ogala is classified as easy to moderate primarily because the trail rolls along without any major climbs and the route is fairly easy to

Getting There

☞ From Columbus – Take **Hwy 46 West** approximately 13 miles to **Hwy 135 South**. Take **Hwy 135 South** 16.3 miles to **County Road 1190 North**. This is the **first left** you can take once you cross the **Jackson County Line**. Turn **left** on **County Road 1190 North** (follow the bends to the right and to the left) and travel 1.1 miles to the **parking area**.

navigate. There are a couple of challenging climbs at the east end of the route that make the ride a little more intense.

One of the first points of interest cyclists will come across is Sundance Lake (*you actually pass the entrance leading to Sundance Lake*). Named after a Native American purification ceremony, the lake plays host to an annual gathering in late spring. Indians travel from around the country to attend this ancient dance. Strict rules apply and no photographs or video may be taken. Guards are posted throughout the woods to enforce this rule. A local resident tells of a TV crew that was escorted out of the woods when they were caught with their cameras and equipment. Strict policies aside, guests are welcome to attend. More information can be obtained from the Hoosier National Forest Offices.

Sundance Lake is also known for its fishing. If you can tote a pole while you ride, it might be worth the effort. This 5.3-acre lake was built in 1992 with the cooperation of Indiana's B.A.S.S. (Bass Anglers Sportsman Society) Chapter Federation, Indiana's Department of Natural Resources, Soil Conservation Service, and the Forest Service. This consorted effort created one of Hoosier National Forest's most productive lakes. Stocked with redear, bluegill, bass, and channel catfish, almost anyone can catch a fish here.

Once past Sundance, cyclists will pass off the dirt road and return to singletrack. Dropping down into a hollow, cyclists then bottom out at a series of recovering ravines. These gullies reveal the sad shape this land was in before being purchased by the Forest Service. The four-foot gullies have stabilized from the grass and small trees that have dropped roots here. However, this section still is unrideable, and cyclists will have to shoulder their bikes to continue the route.

From here the trail flattens out for a short distance while leading to the route's notable climbs. At the east end of the trail, the path rolls over

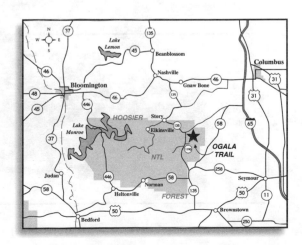

two ridges before turning back to the west. Just past this bend, the path passes an abandoned storage building and bends back to the north. Soon after this turn, the trail steadily climbs and turns, continuing its trek west. In the winter, when the brush is low, cyclists are offered a scenic view of the adjacent ridge from the top of this climb.

The final leg of Ogala follows County Road 1190 North. As a bonus, a high-speed downhill offers a grand finale that carries cyclists into the parking area.

Once the bikes are on the rack, relaxation is found just one mile from the trailhead. Comfortable beds and a continental breakfast await at the Blossom Hollow Bed and Breakfast. The downside to these quarters is that there are only two rooms. Therefore, it's best to call ahead for reservations. The upside, however, if you are lucky enough to get a room in May, comes when the dogwoods are in full-bloom. The white blooms of the trees fill the hollow and paints a glorious springtime scene.

Ogala is open to hunters, has great fishing, hosts a large Native American gathering, is home to a number of feathered friends for bird watchers to enjoy, and has a quaint bed and breakfast close by, yet it remains fairly anonymous. I guess word of this outdoor jewel just hasn't gotten out to the public — yet.

MILES	DIRECTIONS
0.0	**START** from the **parking area** off **1190 North Road**. Leave the parking area and roll past the gate at the north end of the parking area.
0.1	The trail crosses a small creek.
0.2	The trail splits. Take the **left split**.
0.8	The trail splits. In the summer, this split is difficult to see. Take the **left split** and **cross a creek**. A blue marker is on the near side

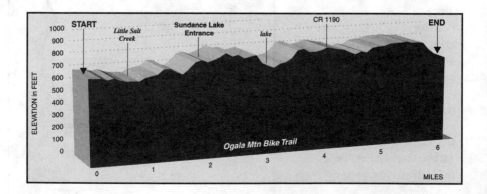

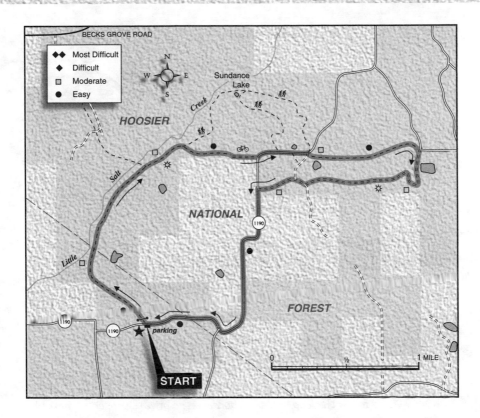

of the creek. A white diamond can be seen on the opposite side of the creek.

1.1 The trail splits. Take the **right split**. The left split crosses **Little Salt Creek** and leads to Becks Grove Road.

1.4 Arrive at a **trail intersection** marked by a brown **HNF** sign. There is an arrow to the left and two unmarked trails to the right. Continue **straight** through this intersection.

1.5 The trail bends to the left and crosses a small creek. After a small climb, the trail bends to the right, then bends to the left again. These switchbacks are not on the map.

1.8   The trail passes a **deer pond** on the left.

2.0   The trail intersects with **CR 1190 North** at a bend in the road. Turn **left** on CR 1190 NORTH.

2.2   The trail passes the entrance to **Sundance Lake**.

2.3   Turn **right** off **CR 1190 North** into an unmarked parking area for a small unnamed lake. Take an immediate **left** on a faded, downhill forest road heading east.

2.4   Arrive at a series of **deep gullies**. This is an example of the massive erosion that occurred before HNF purchased the land. Shoulder your bike and cross the four-foot gullies and continue straight.

2.5   Arrive at a **trail intersection**. Turn **left**. The trail immediately bends to the right and parallels an abandoned forest road. The trail basically follows the old forest road to a dirt road.

3.0   The trail crosses over the end of a dirt road. Cross the dirt road and follow the jeep trail that borders the private property (marked by two ten-foot posts, each with "No Trespassing" signs) on the left. Pass a lake and climb over a ridge.

3.2   Pass a trail on the left. Continue **straight**.

Ride Information

Trail Maintenance Hotline:

Hoosier National Forest	(812) 275-5987
811 Constitution Ave.	
Bedford, IN 47421	
Brownstown Ranger District	(812) 358-2675
608 W. Commerce Street	
Brownstown, IN 47420	

Accommodations:

Blossom Bed and Breakfast	(812) 988-9374
9989 State Road 135 South	
Freetown, IN 47235	

Maps:

USGS map: Waymansville, IN

3.3   Arrive at a **trail intersection**. Turn **right**.

3.35 Pass an abandoned storage building on the left. The trail bends
      right, heading north. A short climb leads to a bend to the left and
      to a steeper climb.

3.6   Now at the top of the climb. This high point offers a nice view of
      adjacent ridge in the winter when the brush is low.

4.1   The trail merges into another trail. Take the trail to the **right**.

4.2   The trail splits. Take the **split to the left**. The trail to the right
      leads back to the unnamed lake that was passed at 2.3 miles. This
      section is very faint.

4.3   Pass a **hunters' tree** stand on the left as the trail bends to the
      right.

4.35 The trail crosses a **small ditch**.

4.5   The trail intersects with **CR 1190 North**. Turn **left**.

4.7   The road bends to the right.

4.8   The road bends to the left.

5.3   The road bends to the right.

5.5   The road bends to the right and intersects with **CR 400 West**.
      Continue **straight** on **CR 1190 NORTH**.

6.1   A great downhill run finishes at the parking area. Turn **right** into
      the **parking area**. Ride complete.

| Bicycle Touring Companies |

Fat-Tire Vacations

There are literally dozens of off-road bicycling tour companies offering an incredible variety of guided tours for mountain bikers. On these pay-as-you-pedal, fat-tire vacations, you will have a chance to go places around the globe that only an expert can take you, and your experiences will be so much different than if seen through the window of a tour bus.

From Hut to Hut in the Colorado Rockies or Inn to Inn through Vermont's Green Mountains, there is a tour company for you. Whether you want hard-core singletrack during the day and camping at night, or you want scenic trails followed by a bottle of wine at night and a mint on each pillow, someone out there offers what you're looking for. The tours are well organized and fully-supported with expert guides, bike mechanics, "sag wagons," which carry gear, food, and tired bodies. Prices range from $100-$500 for a weekend to more than $2000 for two-week-long trips to far-off lands such as New Zealand or Ireland. Each of these companies will gladly send you their free literature to whet your appetites with breathtaking photography and titillating stories of each of their tours.

Selected Touring Companies

• Elk River Touring Center	Slatyfork, WV	(304) 572-3771
• Vermont Bicycling Touring	Bristol, VT	1-800-245-3868
• Backroads	Berkley, CA	1-800-BIKE-TRIP
• Timberline Bicycle Tours	Denver, CO	(303) 759-3804
• Roads Less Traveled	Longmont, CO	(303) 678-8750
• Blackwater Bikes	Davis, WV	(304) 259-5286
• Bicycle Adventures	Olympia, WA	1-800-443-6060
• Trails Unlimited, Inc.	Nashville, IN	(812) 988-6232

Repair and Maintain

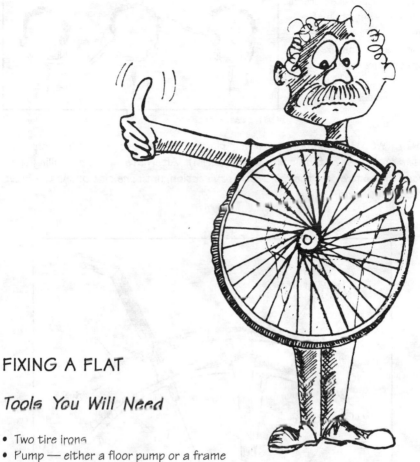

FIXING A FLAT

Tools You Will Need

- Two tire irons
- Pump — either a floor pump or a frame pump
- *No screwdrivers!!!* — This can puncture the tube

Removing the Wheel

The front wheel is easy. Simply open the quick release mechanism or undo the bolts with the proper sized wrench, then remove the wheel from the bike.

The rear wheel is a little more tricky. Before you loosen the wheel from the frame, shift the chain into the smallest gear on the freewheel (the cluster of gears in the back). Once you've done this, removing and installing the wheel, like the front, is much easier.

Removing the Tire

STEP ONE: Make sure all the air is out of the tire. Insert a tire iron under the bead of the tire and pry the tire over the lip of the rim. Be careful not to pinch the tube when you do this.

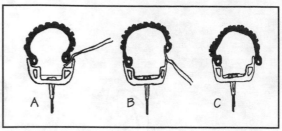

Pull the bead off the rim.

STEP TWO: Hold the first tire iron in place. With the second tire iron, repeat *step one* (three or four inches down the rim). Alternate tire irons, pulling the bead of the tire over the rim, section by section, until one side of the tire bead is completely off the rim.

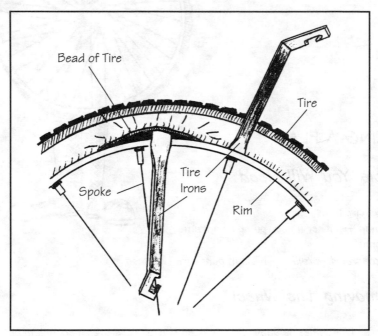

Using tire irons.

STEP THREE: Remove the rest of the tire and tube from the rim. This can be done by hand. It's easiest to remove the valve stem last. Once the tire is off the rim, pull the tube out of the tire.

Clean and Safety Check

STEP FOUR: Using a rag, wipe the inside of the tire to clean out any dirt, sand, glass, thorns, etc. These may cause the tube to puncture. The inside of a tire should feel smooth. Any pricks or bumps could mean that you have found the culprit responsible for your flat tire.

STEP FIVE: Wipe the rim clean, then check the rim strip, making sure it covers the spoke nipples properly on the inside of the rim. If a spoke is poking through the rim strip, it could cause a puncture.

STEP SIX: At this point, you can do one of two things: replace the punctured tube with a new one, or patch the hole. It's easiest to just replace the tube with a new tube when you're out on the trails. Roll up the old tube and take it home to repair later that night in front of the TV. Directions on patching a tube are usually included with the patch kit itself.

Installing the Tire and Tube
(This can be done entirely by hand)

STEP SEVEN: Inflate the new or repaired tube with enough air to give it shape, then tuck it back into the tire.

STEP EIGHT: To put the tire and tube back on the rim, begin by putting the valve in the valve hole. The valve must be straight. Then use your hands to push the beaded edge of the tire onto the rim all the way around so that one side of your tire is on the rim.

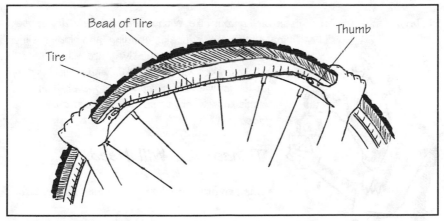

Wrestling a tire onto a rim.

STEP NINE: Let most of the air out of the tube to allow room for the rest of the tire.

STEP TEN: Beginning opposite the valve, use your thumbs to push the other side of the tire onto the rim. Be careful not to pinch the tube in between the tire and the rim. The last few inches may be difficult, and you may need the tire iron to pry the tire onto the rim. If so, just be careful not to puncture the tube.

Before Inflating Completely

STEP ELEVEN: Check to make sure the tire is seated properly and that the tube is not caught between the tire and the rim. Do this by adding about 5 to 10 pounds of air, and watch closely that the tube does not bulge out of the tire.

STEP TWELVE: Once you're sure the tire and tube are properly seated, put the wheel back on the bike, then fill the tire with air. It's easier squeezing the wheel through the brake shoes if the tire is still flat.

STEP THIRTEEN: Now fill the tire with the proper amount of air, and check constantly to make sure the tube doesn't bulge from the rim. If the tube does appear to bulge out, release all the air as quickly as possible, or you could be in for a big bang.

When installing the rear wheel, place the chain back onto the smallest cog (furthest gear on the right), and pull the derailleur out of the way. Your wheel should slide right on.

LUBRICATION AVOIDS DETERIORATION

Lubrication is crucial to maintaining your bike. With a good lube-job, dry spots will be eliminated. Creaks, squeaks, grinding, and binding will be gone. The chain will run quietly, gears will shift smoothly, brakes will grip quicker, and your bike may last longer with fewer repairs. However, if you don't know where to put the lubrication, what good is it?

Things You Will Need

• One can of bicycle lubricant, found at any bike store.
• A clean rag (to wipe excess lubricant away).

What Gets Lubricated

- Front derailleur
- Rear derailleur
- Shift levers
- Front brake
- Rear brake
- Both brake levers
- Chain

Where To Lubricate

To make it easy, simply spray a little lubricant on all the pivot points of your bike. If you're using a squeeze bottle, use just a drop or two. Put a few drops on each point wherever metal moves against metal, for instance, at the center of the brake calipers. Then let the lube sink in.

Once you have applied the lubricant to the derailleurs, shift the gears a few times, working the derailleurs back and forth. This allows the lubricant to work itself into the tiny cracks and spaces it must occupy to do its job. Work the brakes a few times as well.

Lubing The Chain

Lubricating the chain should be done after the chain has been wiped clean of most road grime. Do this by spinning the pedals counterclockwise while gripping the chain with a clean rag. As you add the lubricant, be sure to get some in between each link. With an aerosol spray, just spray the chain while pedalling backwards (counterclockwise) until the chain is fully lubricated. Let the lubricant soak in for a few seconds before wiping the excess away. Chains will collect dirt much faster if they're loaded with too much lubrication.

Indiana Bicycle Clubs and Trail Groups

Mountain Bikes have made a real impact on fighting crime.

IBC (Indiana Bicycle Coalition)
3649 Cold Springs Rd.
Indianapolis, IN 46222
1-800-920-1405
(317) 327-7224

IMBA (International Mountain Bike
Association)
P.O. Box 7578
Boulder, CO 80306
(303) 545-9011

NORBA (National Off Road Bicycle
Association)
1750 East Boulder Street
Colorado Springs, CO 80909
(719) 578-4581

Rails-To-Trails Conservancy
1400 16th Street, NW, Suite 300
Washington, D.C. 20036-2222
(202) 797-5400

League of American Bicyclists
190 West Ostend Street #120
Baltimore, MD 21230-3731
(410) 539-3399

Hoosier Rails-to-Trails Council
P.O. Box 402
Indianapolis, IN 46206-0402
(317) 237-9348

Berne Bicycle Club
266 IN Street
Berne, IN 46711
(219) 724-2705

Blazing Saddles Bicycle Club
P.O. Box 4262
209 W. Jefferson
Decatur, IN 46733
(219) 724-2705

Bloomington Bicycle Club
P.O. Box 463
Bloomington, IN 47402-0463

Break-Away Bicycle Club
P.O. Box 6906
Kokomo, IN 46904-6906
(317) 453-4270

Calumet Crank Club
P.O. Box 2202
Valparaiso, IN 46384-2202
(219) 464-4322

Central Indiana Bicycle Assoc.
P.O. Box 55405
Indianapolis, IN 46205
(317) 251-2122

Cincinnati Cycling Club
3005 Aquadale Lane
Cincinnati, OH 45211
(513) 791-7190

Delaware Cycling Club
3205 W. Ivy Street
Muncie, IN 47304
(317) 284-6847

Driftwood Valley Wheelers
P.O. Box 1552
1446 Lafayette Ave.
Columbus, IN 47202
(812) 579-6075

Evansville Masters Bike Club
532 Runnymeade Ave.
Evansville, IN 47714

Evansville Bicycle Club
3121 Woodview Ct. #238
Evansville, IN 47715-8060

Evansville Road Riders
616 W. Mt. Pleasant Rd.
Evansville, IN 47711
(812) 867-5280

Exiles Cycling Club
1234 N. Main St.
Crown Point, IN 46307
(219) 362-8383

Folks on Spokes
P.O. Box 824
Homewood, IL 60430-0824

GA BA Bike Club
P.O. Box 682
New Castle, IN 47362

Huntington County Wheelers
226 Randolph St.
Huntington, IN 46750
(219) 356-2606

Int. Human Powered Vehicle Assoc.
P.O. Box 51255
Indianapolis, IN 46251
(317) 876-9478

Jayland Sprockets
R.R. 5 Box 34
Portland, IN 47371

Maple City Bicycle Club
P.O. Box 55
Laporte, IN 46350-4200
(219) 362-4200

Michiana Bicycling Association
P.O. Box 182
Granger, IN 46530-0182
(616) 695-9591

Northwest Indiana AYH
8231 Lake Shore Drive
Gary, IN 46403-0016
(219) 374-7160

Ohio Valley Bicycle Club
Box 165
Derby, IN 47525
(812) 843-5416

Plymouth Pedal Pushers
P.O. Box 387
Plymouth, IN 46563-0387

Richmond Cycling Club
P.O. Box 3
Pershing, IN 47370
(317) 478-3656

Saddle Sore Cruisers
1242 Upper 11th
Vincennes, IN 47591
(812) 882-8911

Slow Spokes of Indiana
511 Oakwood St.
Angola, IN 46703
(219) 665-9391

Southern Indiana Wheelmen
111 Hwy 131
Clarksville, IN 47129
(812) 944-2762

Spoke & Wheel Bicycle Club
5851 W. 200 N
Anderson, IN 46011-9146
(317) 643-7498

Terre Haute Touring Cyclists
2535 N. 9th
Terre Haute, IN 47804

The Rose Pedals
5500 Wabash Ave.
Terre Haute, IN 47803

Three Rivers Velo Sport
P.O. Box 11391
Fort Wayne, IN 46857-1139

TRAIL
6460 Shelbyville Road
Indianapolis, IN 46237

Wabash River Cycle Club
360 Brown Street
West Lafayette, IN 47906-3212
(317) 743-3506

Wandering Wheels
P.O. Box 207
Upland, IN 46989
(317) 998-7490

Wesley Wheelers
P.O. Box 28
Daleville, IN 47334

Wheel People Bicycle Assoc.
R.R. #1, Box 164
Galveston, IN 46932
(219) 699-6825

Index

About the Author

Layne Cameron, a native of Indiana, has been involved in bicycle racing and recreation for many years. When he's not writing articles for *VeloNews*, *Bicycling*, *Sports Illustrated for Kids*, or writing and editing regular columns for various children's magazines, Layne can usually be found conquering new and uncharted Hoosier singletrack, spinning thin tires at the Major Taylor Velodrome, or jumping into impromptu group rides near his home in Indianapolis.

Other available guides in
Beachway Press'
Mountain Bike America
series

Ask for these books at your local bookstore or outdoor store

— or —

order them directly from

Beachway Press
9201 Beachway Lane
Springfield, VA 22153-1441

include $2.00 shipping per item

BarMap© and BarMap OTG©
by CycoActive PRODUCTS

Don't mangle this book on the first ride!

While *Mountain Bike Indiana* may be the quickest way to learn the area, carrying it and paging through it on a ride will get old fast—pages will get dirty, the cover will bend, and this book will never look good on your bookshelf again.

Put a copy of the map on the front side.

Enter the **BarMap®**. The BarMap mapcase is a simple, lightweight solution to this age-old problem many guidebook owners often experience. Its soft, clear mapcase velcros easily to the handlebar and those days of digging maps out of your fanny pack, unfolding, refolding, and stuffing them back in, are forever in the past. Get the loop right the first time and leave the book in the car! Item # BM-SV: **$7.95**

Item # BM-SV

Put a copy of the directions on the back side.

The **BarMap OTG®** *(Of The Gods)* attaches to the bar and stem with three velcro loops. This compact carrying case shows an entire 8½" x 11" map inside, yet folds to a compact 5" x 6" on the stem, slightly larger than a wallet. There's a 4" x 5" clear pocket on the outside for route instructions. Inside is a mesh pocket for keys or money, and another pocket for energy bars or a notepad and pen. Sewn of Cordura® and clear vinyl, with nylon borders. Item # BM-OTGV: **$19.95**

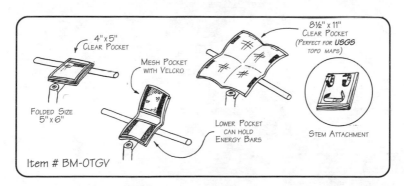

4" x 5" CLEAR POCKET

MESH POCKET WITH VELCRO

8½" x 11" CLEAR POCKET (PERFECT FOR USGS TOPO MAPS)

FOLDED SIZE 5" x 6"

LOWER POCKET CAN HOLD ENERGY BARS

STEM ATTACHMENT

Item # BM-OTGV

To order—send check or money order to:

add $2.00 shipping for each item

Beachway Press
9201 Beachway Lane
Springfield, VA 22153
(703) 644-8544

...or ask dealer to stock products

Be sure to include **item #** with order